ENIGMATIC ENGLAND

To our parents, Eve and Os Crouch, and Peter and Ray Meers who started our love of history, landscape, and architecture.

PADDY'S HOLE, MIDDLESBOROUGH

ENIGMATIC ENGLAND

NICK MEERS & SUE SEDDON

ALAN SUTTON

First published in the United Kingdom in 1990 by

Alan Sutton Publishing Ltd · Phoenix Mill · Far Thrupp · Stroud · Gloucestershire

First published in the United States of America in 1991 by

Alan Sutton Publishing Inc · Wolfeboro Falls · NH 3896–0848

British Library Cataloguing in Publication Data

Meers, Nick, *1955*–
    Enigmatic England.
    1. England. Description & travel
    I. Title   II. Seddon, Sue
    914.204859

    ISBN 0–86299–626–0

Library of Congress Cataloging in Publication Data

Meers, Nick *1955*–
    Enigmatic England / Nick Meers, Sue Seddon.
        p.   cm.
    ISBN 0–86299–626–0 : $32.00
    1. England -- Description and travel -- 1991 ---- Views.   I. Seddon,
Sue.   II. Title.
    DA667.M44 1991   90–45839
    942--dc20   CIP

Typeset in 9½/15pt Bembo.
Typesetting and origination by
Alan Sutton Publishing Limited.
Colour separation by Yeo Valley Graphic Reproductions, Wells.
Printed in Italy by New Interlitho S.p.A., Milan.

SHAKESPEARE'S BIRTHPLACE,

STRATFORD-UPON-AVON

CONTENTS

INTRODUCTION

An enigma is something that is mysterious, puzzling or ambiguous, but there was nothing enigmatic about the situation when the car broke down in the pouring rain at four in the morning on our third attempt to photograph dawn over Avebury. The only enigma that day was the sun. But the weather improved as we travelled the country and what became increasingly enigmatic was England itself.

We set out to capture some of the quirks and surprises that are quintessentially English. We thought we knew quite a lot of them, but as one discovery led to another we were astonished and intrigued by their number and variety. In cities and in the country we found a rich vein of contrasts where the juxtaposition of buildings or landscapes kept us hooked on the hunt.

Some of the places in the book are well known and we have taken a new look at these and shown them from a point of view that isn't often seen; others are almost unknown outside their locality. To sustain the element of surprise each location has been photographed three times. The first picture of each sequence is a detail which gives little away about the identity of the location and aims to get the reader guessing; the second is a mid-shot which gives more clues, and the third is the denouement: a panoramic shot of the subject in its setting.

It is, of course, a subjective view of England and includes quirks, humour, history, anecdotes, grandeur, beauty, and sometimes the downright appalling. But the last is very much part of our view. Each place is real and set in its context; we wanted to show things as they really are, even if a motorway carved up a beautiful landscape or a shopping precinct dwarfed a medieval building.

Although such planning atrocities exist, our journey through England has given us many more highs than lows: landscapes to move the heart, buildings that are touching survivors of another age, and endless examples of people's ingenuity and vision. Our odyssey turned into a pilgrimage and made two confirmed Anglophiles even more enthusiastic about the quiet surprises which make England so richly enigmatic.

NICK MEERS & SUE SEDDON
October 1990

'To Virtue only & her friends a Friend,
The World besides may blame or may Commend,
All the malicious Lies that World can raise
Disturb me not, I Count its censure praise.'

EP, 1770

'————a settled Virtue
makes itself Judge, & satisfied within,
Smiles at that Common Enemy, the World————'

'Defleo Praeteritae Cimissa Piacula Vitae
Flagrat et Aeterni pectus amore Dei'
[I weep for sins committed in my past life
and my heart burns with love of eternal God]

Some of England's most elegant graffiti is scratched on the imposing windows of a great Elizabethan country house. The contemplative lines were done in the eighteenth century and are strangely at odds with their location, for they renounce worldy matters but are written on one of the great status symbols of the materialistic Elizabethan Age – the window. Who so defied the grandeur of his inheritance and committed his thoughts to glass?

The Phelips family lived at Montacute House in Somerset for over three hundred years and it was Edward Phelips (1725–97), the fifth of that name, who etched the panes of the Great Chamber or library window. It was not some naughty schoolboy prank as Edward Phelips was forty-five and master of the house when he wrote the verse dated 1770 on the window. Records show him to have been a kindly man who cared for his family, servants, estate workers and tenants. He trained as a lawyer and became an MP through a sense of duty rather than a love of politics, complaining about the number of committees he was forced to attend. He would much rather have been in Somerset

hunting with his friends. When he inherited the estate in 1750 it was beset with debt but he proved to be an excellent manager and, with the help of some bequests, enabled Montacute to flourish again.

At about the time of Edward's birth the family's fortunes had declined so far that they could not afford to heat the Great Chamber in the north wing, so it was shut off and used as a store room. An inventory of 1728 shows that it was used to store tables, stools, chests, chairs, several family portraits, 'Sundry boxes and a Trunk not looked into, A quantity of Dry Elm board, A quantity of Wallnut plank & severall other Lumber Goods'. At some point during Edward's life the room was cleared of its junk and turned into a library. This may well have been Edward's doing as he made many improvements to the house. Junk room or library, either use might have inspired him to write on the windows. We have no means of knowing what instrument he used, but it is a romantic thought that he might have used a diamond.

The stained glass coats of arms on the library windows were an Elizabethan

device designed to impress. As well as the arms of the Phelips family (top row, second from left, parted with the Horsey arms), there are the arms of Somerset neighbours; noble families – Devereux, Earl of Essex, for example; eminent statesmen, and the arms of members of the royal family. Glass, especially stained glass, was still an expensive luxury when Montacute was completed in 1601 and the size and number of its glittering windows indicate the wealth of its owner.

Montacute is an exquisite house, its gables, turrets, tall chimneys, windows, columns, parapets and garden pavilions give it an air of fantasy that lifts it out of the ordinary. When the evening sun lights the honey-coloured Ham Hill stone it glows, the perfect setting for a masque of Elizabethan faeries.

Although Edward Phelips was heir to such grandeur and cared greatly for the house, the graffiti on the library windows show him to have been pensive about the world. He must have spent many quiet hours of reflection in his library before he etched his thoughts on the panes of glass. He had studied the classics and in 1770 he laboriously scratched in Latin:

'Happy is the man with the keen intellect and superhuman eagerness to reveal the innermost secrets of nature; happy is he who can grasp the causes and relationships of matter; who can walk in the footsteps of Newton as his companion. But happy too is the man who cares for his fields; who appreciates all the manifold riches of his garden; who has learnt the art of grafting trees that each may thrive in its favourite soil. . . . Do not scorn or grumble about his modest toil; it is shared by the greatest gardener of all. Do not look for him only amid the stars of heaven; for it is in the ordinary things of life that you may find God.'

                    1770 Garden of Eden

MONTACUTE HOUSE, MONTACUTE, SOMERSET

'*Not without Art, but yet to Nature true,*
She charms the town with humour just, yet new.'

CHARLES CHURCHILL

Deep in the green water meadows a small herd of Friesians and their calves graze an English pasture. It is a typical idyll, or would be if the creatures were flesh and blood, but these op art animals are clearly not warm blooded: from head to hoof they are made of concrete. Browsing beside the main London to Glasgow railway line they might be a Milk Marketing Board advertizement, but these are The Concrete Cows, a work of public art and pride of Milton Keynes.

Liz Leyh, the American sculptor and artist in residence to Milton Keynes schools, made them as a parting gift for the town in 1978. Initially they were the butt of bovine jokes, but after a while the residents took them to heart and by 1987 their affection for the six cows had grown so much that they held a tenth anniversary party for them. So it was with great consternation that Milton Keynes awoke one morning to find that one of its cows was missing.

Overnight someone had taken a stone-cutter to one of the calves and felled it just above the fetlocks. There was no sign of it. Heaven knows why or how it was removed as it weighs about 200 kilograms, but it had completely disappeared. Milton Keynes resigned itself to a madman's prank and prepared to take a pride in the remaining five cows.

That was the situation until a Milton Keynes resident went to a summer fair in Cambridge and there on the banks of the Cam, in amongst the parked cars and the general hurly-burly, the amazed resident spotted the calf and alerted the Cambridge constabulary. Now a Milton Keynes resident knows a concrete cow when he sees one but the Cambridge police were, understandably, a little reluctant to give the story full credit. However, they contacted the Milton Keynes police who verified the story, but by the time the Cambridge police reached the Cam-side car park the calf had gone – again.

The case of the missing calf might have rested there, but the morning after the incident a Cambridge resident, blearily opening the curtains, was astonished to find a Friesian calf on his front lawn. He contacted the police thinking that they were never going to believe him, but of course they did. The maddest cow in Milton Keynes was returned to its home town and when it has been repaired it will gambol once more beside the railway line.

New towns are orderly places, the planners see to that. Residential and business areas are kept apart, cars and pedestrians are separated. In central Milton Keynes all the food shops are under one roof – the Food Centre, while other stores are in the Shopping Building. Grass, mown to tennis-lawn smoothness, covers the open spaces between the residential areas like a fitted carpet. Although more than thirteen million trees and shrubs have been planted the town has a close-shaven neatness that makes old-town dwellers wince.

Official brochures about Milton Keynes are breathless with achievement. Since building began in 1971 over forty thousand new homes have been built and the population has reached nearly 145,000. Hundreds of businesses have moved to the town, including so many Japanese companies that Milton Keynes has appointed an Anglo–Japanese Liaison Officer, and a Japanese boarding school has been built. There are leisure palaces where residents can take their ease or exercise. In spite of all these facilities new towns are still regarded by many people as the last place on earth they would choose to live and this is their enigma: their very newness makes them seem inhospitable and bland, but the creation of a new town is a bold and exciting achievement which gives them vibrance. Given time, perhaps we will come to regard them with affection, just as the residents took to heart the Milton Keynes Cows.

THE COWS, MILTON KEYNES, BUCKINGHAMSHIRE

'Teetotal Moses struck the rock,
And water gushed therefrom;
But Peter yields John Barleycorn
And good old English Tom.'

Attr. BILLY MITFORD

To get a pint in Marsden takes some nerve: to reach the pub you have to step off the top of a cliff and make the descent in a lift. The Grotto is one of the most curious public houses in England. It appears to be a 1930s building nestling at the foot of the cliff in Marsden Bay, near South Shields, Tyne and Wear, but a closer look reveals how it got its name – much of it is hollowed out of the cliff.

The present frontage and lift were built by the Vaux Company when it bought the old inn in 1938. The lift opens into the lounge bar, the front wall of which is a conventional room, but at the back is a white painted grotto. Openings lead into several smaller rooms which are also caves, and there is a restaurant upstairs, decorated like a sultan's tent. The whole effect is rather bizarre and would be totally unrecognizable to the man who originally hewed the caves out of the cliff.

There were natural caves in the cliffs of this wild and beautiful stretch of coast, which are said to have been the haunt of smugglers and ghosts. In 1782 a local character known as Jack the Blaster, who had been a poacher, smuggler and quarryman, retired to live in one of the caves with his wife. He was then aged eighty and many people came to see the quaint old couple who lived in the caves. Jack and his wife sold refreshments to their nosy visitors.

It was Peter Allan, an entrepreneur of vision and optimism, who developed the idea. Allan came to Marsden in 1830 and saw the potential of providing refreshment to the many visitors who stopped at the bay. He had been a valet, gamekeeper and foreman of a quarrying company before he hit upon the idea of making a house and an inn by cutting caves in the cliff. When he won some money at Shields races he bought a tent and sold refreshments from it while he began the arduous task of enlarging and excavating caves in which to live and run his business.

Eventually there were fifteen rooms on two storeys. Some of the rooms had balconies where visitors could sit and drink a beer while enjoying the coastal scenery. Allan had had a long struggle to obtain a licence for his caves as local excise men suspected him of being a glorified smuggler. There was also a ballroom where dancers could waltz away the night.

At first, Mr and Mrs Allan and their eight children, five sons and three daughters, lived in the caves during the summer and returned to the dryer and safer village of Whitburn in the winter. But somehow Peter managed to persuade his family to live in the caves all year round. It can be a wild coast and the waves sometimes broke through the door and flooded their troglodytic house. On one occasion their two-year-old was swept up by a huge wave which had burst into the cave. The poor little thing was saved by one of its brothers who scooped it up just as the wave was sucking it out to sea.

Peter lived in the caves with his family and entourage of pets – tame pigs and ravens, doves in the cliff dovecote and bees in the bar – for twenty-two years. He was known for miles around and his inn was always popular, but he had no legal claim to the site and was a squatter. When the land about him was bought up in 1849 the new owner demanded rent. Peter refused and went to court to fight for his demesne, but the court case went against him and, heartbroken, he went into a depression and refused to eat. He died on 31 August 1849, aged fifty-one. His wife and son William agreed to pay the rent and continued at the Grotto until 1874, when the lease expired. Over thirty-five years they had served thousands of customers and the Grotto was so well-established that it continued to be an inn.

Before the Vaux Company took the lease in 1898 there had been several other leaseholders, some of whom were almost as colourful as Peter Allan. Until the lift was built it was a difficult place to run as all supplies had to be lowered over the cliff by winch. Customers reached the inn by a precipitous zig-zag path which must have been hazardous after a good night out.

It is not the inn alone which draws so many people to Marsden Bay. Although mines, caravan sites and housing estates scar the land nearby, the coast itself is beautiful. The Grotto shares the bay with Marsden Rock, a magnificent weathered sea-stack of magnesian limestone, 33.2 metres high, through which the sea has carved a great cathedral arch. It is so near the cliffs that at the lift entrance you are level with its top and can see some of the hundreds of seabirds which nest there. From the sands Marsden Rock is compelling and the air is filled with the cries of kittiwakes, gulls and cormorants.

THE GROTTO AND MARSDEN ROCK, TYNE AND WEAR

'. . . upon this rock I will build my church;
and the gates of hell shall not prevail against it.'

ST MATTHEW 15:18

Three columns of rock stretch upward from a mound, topped by a ruined chapel. They rise so dramatically from the ground that they could be in the Languedoc or on a Mediterranean island. In fact this is England, Cornwall to be precise, and well inland.

Roche Rock smells ancient. Its lichen-spattered boulders and craggy pinnacles give off an air of battles fought with dark powers before time was measured in hours. Perhaps it was to keep up the good fight that a chapel was built on top of the central rock at the beginning of the fifteenth century. Perched high off the ground the building takes root in the rock, which also forms one of the walls of the chapel. The top of the rock is almost 25 sheer metres from the ground and building the chapel must have been an act of faith.

The lower room is traditionally said to have been a hermit's cell, but more likely to have been a room for the chaplain who used to celebrate St Michael's Day in the tiny chapel above. The chapel was licensed on 16 September 1409, and dedicated to St Michael, who must have had a good head for heights as many chapels in high places, such as Mont St Michel and St Michael's Mount, were dedicated to him in the Middle Ages.

Cornish folklore has woven Roche Rock into its stories. Tregeagle, the hapless Cornish spirit who was set the impossible task of draining Dozmary Pool with a leaky limpet shell gave up the hopeless task and, pursued by screaming devils, fled howling across the moors to Roche Rock, where he sought comfort and sanctuary from the hermit who lived there. Apparently the legendary spirit did not like the holy words of the hermit any better than the screams of the devils at his heels, and on dark nights when the wind storms around the Rock, Tregeagle can still be heard howling his despair above the wind.

There are so many references to the hermit of Roche Rock that it seems likely that there was one. Some say that he was St Gonand, to whom the church in the nearby village of Roche is dedicated. He is traditionally said to have been a leper. If he did exist, then his view from the top of the rock must have been less startling and more green than it is today.

South of the rock is a ruinous landscape of spoil heaps, the result of the china clay mining industry. Until the eighteenth century the secret of making porcelain had been closely kept by the Chinese for centuries. A wholesale chemist from Plymouth, William Cookworthy (1705–80) broke the spell by studying an account of the Chinese technique of making porcelain given by a Jesuit priest. Cookworthy set about finding the necessary deposits of china clay in Cornwall. His diligence paid off when he found that the area around St Austell was rich with the right clay, and after some experimental years he patented the method in 1768. From then on the industry took off. The Midland potteries began to make porcelain and quantities of china clay were shipped from Cornwall to Staffordshire.

The industry now produces about 3 million tonnes of china clay a year, but the process of extracting it makes vast amounts of sand (about 10 million tonnes annually) and mica waste. The sand is piled in huge tips which have been named the 'Cornish Alps', although since the disaster at Aberfan in 1966 all tips must be flat-topped by law. The clay mining industry is trying to find ways of landscaping these man-made mountains to restore the ravaged landscape. The tips are gradually being seeded and the mica waste is no longer poured into the local rivers, but fed into storage lagoons which will eventually be planted. Research and landscaping has so far cost about £12 million and the industry will continue to spend about £750,000 a year on the project.

Although it is about 207 metres above sea level, Roche Rock is dwarfed by the towering china clay workings to the south. They are unearthly and would be more at home in a science fiction film than in the Cornish countryside. It will be years before they are green again but until then Roche Rock is an outcrop of reality set bravely against a surreal backdrop.

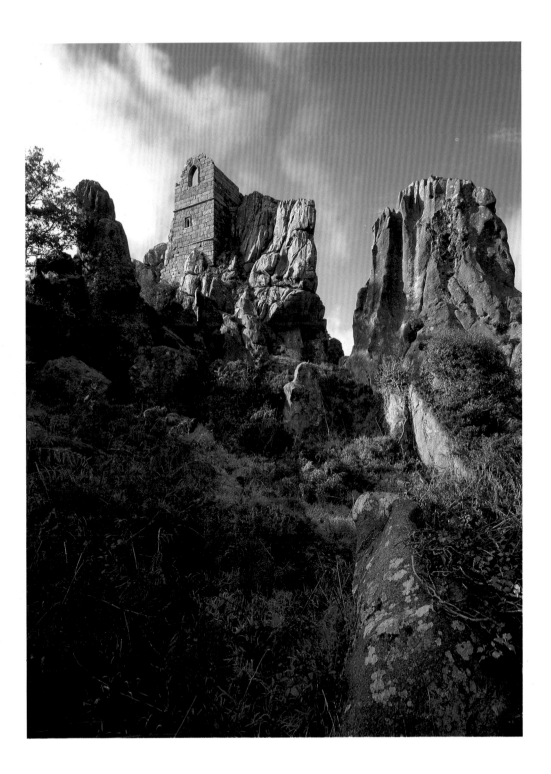

ROCHE ROCK, ROCHE, CORNWALL

'God does not play dice.'

EINSTEIN'S REACTION TO
THE QUANTUM THEORY

Frozen in mid-play three dice are cast in an unexpected setting. These secular symbols have hung above the high altar of Winchester Cathedral for 400 years. They are just one of over a thousand roof bosses found in the soaring heights of the cathedral's magnificent roof.

The dice are part of a set of thirty Passion emblems depicting events and objects connected with Christ's Passion. The dice represent the story of the Roman soldiers who cast lots for Christ's raiment at the foot of the cross. Bishop Fox, who commissioned them in about 1506, wanted to add to the impressive stonework of the cathedral but had to be content with a new wooden roof in the choir as the walls would not support the weight of stone vaulting. At first glance the vaulting, 21.6 metres above the ground, looks as if it is stone, just as Bishop Fox intended.

That all is not as it seems is a recurrent theme at Winchester. Crouched at the centre of the town the cathedral seems eternally solid and indestructible, the epitome of a house built on rock, but it almost sank without trace at the beginning of the twentieth century. A deep sea diver saved it.

Set in a hollow, the cathedral's foundations are prone to winter floods, the Norman builders of 1079 tried to get round the problem by constructing it on a massive wooden raft. This bit of eleventh-century engineering was doomed to fail and 800 years later the cathedral was literally sinking below the earth's surface. William Walker, an intrepid deep sea diver, was employed to creep about the foundations of the building in the slimy blackness, underpinning the walls with 25,800 bags of concrete and 900,000 bricks. His gallant sucess is commemorated by a statue in the cathedral which he saved.

The nave is Winchester's great glory. It is the longest nave in the Western world and soars upwards to 24 metres, the vaulting lit through the delicate perpendicular clerestory. It is a magnificent example of late Gothic architecture, but it was not always so: the elegant perpendicular columns, arches, roof and vaulting seen today are, in fact, a stone casing which covers the original Norman architecture. It seems that the bishops of the fourteenth century were as prone to changing fashions and styles in architecture as we are. Bishop William of

Edington began the process of 'modernizing' the nave of Winchester in the middle of the fourteenth century, but most of the work was carried out under the guidance of the brilliant and energetic William of Wykeham who was Bishop of Winchester between 1366 and 1404. Clambering about in the roof space above the nave today, it is still possible to see some of the original Norman beams and stonework. The transepts escaped remodelling and give a good idea of how the Norman cathedral must have looked.

We have grown accustomed to the subtle colour of natural stone that dominates English cathedrals, but medieval and early Renaissance taste was far more gaudy. At Winchester the high altar screen, dated between 1470 and 1476, originally had over fifty painted and gilded statues. The effect of flesh-coloured faces and scarlet, green, blue or gold robes of saints, kings, prophets and bishops, as well as the crucified Christ, must have been a dazzling focus for devotion. However, the colourful splendour of the screen was destroyed at the Reformation. The statues, which were considered to be idolatrous at the time, were taken down from the great screen, the heads and hands were cut off and the bodies sawn into three and used as building blocks or hard core in nearby buildings. Altogether about two hundred images were removed from the cathedral. During nineteenth-century repairs many fragments of the statues with the original pigment still clinging to them were found. They were too badly damaged to be reinstated in their niches on the screen, but they can be seen in the Triforium Gallery in the cathedral. Today, the screen has nineteenth-century figures which seem mawkish in their fifteenth-century setting.

Winchester Cathedral is quintessentially English. Built on the site of a Saxon cathedral, it contains the bones of many Anglo-Saxon kings. Its vaulted spaces have an air of strength, serenity and perpetuity, but its survival depends partly on a game of chance. The upkeep of this, the second longest church in the world, costs £600,000 a year. Much of this vast sum comes from visitors to the cathedral. That the future of this building, which has stood for 900 years, depends partly on the goodwill of tourists, seems almost as chancy as a throw of the dice.

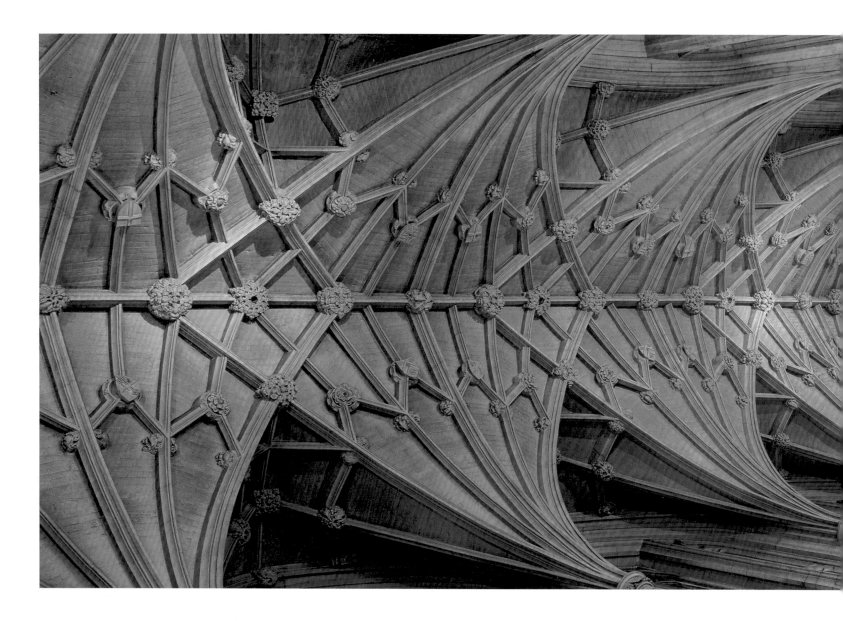

THE NAVE, WINCHESTER CATHEDRAL, HAMPSHIRE

'Had I but plenty of money, money enough and to spare,
The house for me, no doubt, were a house in the city-square.'

ROBERT BROWNING

Built to last, the Old Wellington Inn has stood in a square in the city of Manchester for well over four centuries. The oldest timber building in the city centre, it is a well-known landmark and a popular pub. It has withstood so many onslaughts that it is a small miracle that it still stands.

Originally only two storeys high when it was built in about 1550, radical changes were made in the seventeenth century when the third storey with decorated gables was added. The oak ornamentation on the gables was a speciality of Manchester and Salford town houses, apart from the Old Wellington no others survive in the city. For centuries the unique timber patterns were concealed under a thick coat of plaster and were only revealed when the building was restored in 1976.

Inevitably such an ancient monument has seen many uses. In the sixteenth century it probably housed several shops with living accommodation on the first floor. During the seventeenth century it was converted into an impressive town house. It did not become a pub until 1830, when it was first licensed, and it was

probably given the name 'Old Wellington' in the middle of the last century. Old photographs show that for many decades only the ground floor was used as a pub, the top floors were at first the premises of an optician and mathematical instrument maker, then a fishing tackle shop. A photograph taken in 1866 shows the delicate craftsmanship of the seventeenth century plastered over and hung with a pair of giant spectacles; by 1900 these had been replaced by a clock.

The building has survived many occupants, some of substance: the founder of the city's first bank lived here, as did a founder of Manchester's cotton industry. Other inhabitants financed at least one city church and a hospital. The house was also the birthplace of the inventor of phonetic shorthand. John Byrom was born on 29 February 1692. His family's fortune had been made in the drapery business but John left the running of that to his sister and used his talents to invent a system of shorthand which was the forerunner of Pitman's. He made his living by teaching his system to others, including Horace Walpole and John Wesley.

In the Market Place where the house

stood were the pillory, stocks and market cross, making it the hub of the city. From the windows overlooking the square, in 1745, John Byrom witnessed an historical event which he described in a letter: 'My curiosity led me to my sister's window at the Cross, where I beheld this extraordinary event of two men and a half taking our famous town of Manchester without any resistance or opposition . . .'.

What John Byrom had seen was the taking of Manchester by Bonnie Prince Charlie's troops. The 'two men and a half' were a sergeant, a drummer and a woman: the advance party of the main Highland army which arrived with the Young Pretender the next day. The Jacobite occupation was short-lived, but the house remained in the Byrom family for another eighty-five years.

It survived an even worse attack when the whole of the market place area was devastated by bombs in 1940. Although it escaped destruction its future was not secure. Bombs had failed, but property developers of the 1950s and '60s almost succeeded in demolishing the Old Wellington. Various plans to develop the area were thwarted by public opinion which insisted that the ancient building should remain. Eventually a plan was adopted which was to be the biggest upheaval the building had yet endured.

In 1971 the Old Wellington and the oyster bar next to it were literally raised off the ground by 12.43 metres to make way for a service road to the new development which was to surround them. Braced and cocooned, the 862 tonne buildings were lifted by hydraulic jacks in an extremely delicate operation. The Old Wellington was then expertly restored at great expense and it has been lovingly saved, but at a cost. Viewing it in its present surroundings it is apparent that the property developers of the twentieth century have succeeded where the onslaughts of centuries, the Jacobite Rebellion, and Hitler's bombs failed.

THE OLD WELLINGTON INN, MANCHESTER

'But Sir Richard cried in his English pride,
"We have fought such a fight for a day and a night
As may never be fought again!
We have won great glory, my men!"'

TENNYSON

Rolling pastures sweep towards the cliff edge like a swelling green ocean, breaking where the Atlantic pounds the north coast of Cornwall. This is ancient farmland where sheep crop the turf above the spray buffeted by racing winds. On clear days, walkers on the South-West Coastal Path are rewarded with magnificent seascapes and the exhilaration of walking at the edge of the land, where the ocean stretches uninterrupted to the Americas.

In Cornwall one is never more than about twenty miles from the sea. Perhaps this sense of being at the edge of the realm was one of the reasons why the men of Cornwall and Devon were such bold adventurers and fierce defenders of the kingdom in Elizabethan times. Those swashbuckling heroes Raleigh, Drake and Grenville were all from the south-west peninsula.

The farmland shown here is near Morwenstow, just inside the Cornish border. The Grenville family settled here and farmed the land from about 1200. There was a large medieval house and it was here that Sir Richard Grenville came when he had sold his Devon estate at Buckland Abbey in 1581 to Sir Francis Drake. Drake had triumphantly returned from his circumnavigation and bought Buckland with the spoils. Grenville sold it to him reluctantly because he saw Drake as a parvenu and rival, but, as with many old families, the Grenvilles needed the money. Such was Sir Richard's distaste of the transaction that it was an undercover sale.

Sir Richard Grenville was an active defender of the realm. During the period of national alarm leading up to the Armada he was responsible for the land defence of Cornwall and organized the trained bands of western men who would have to fight off the Spaniards if the unthinkable happened and the great Spanish crusade against heretic England managed to land. Even after the Channel winds had given England victory by scattering the Armada, the threat from Spain remained. Tradition says that when Philip II of Spain received the news of the disaster he remarked, 'I give thanks to God . . . that I can put to sea another fleet as great as this we have lost whenever I choose.' Another Spanish fleet was soon afloat defending the great Spanish treasure fleets on which Spain depended for her wealth and military might. The war continued, much of it at sea where Elizabeth's self-seeking buccaneers, barely disguised as her majesty's respectable defenders of the realm, harried the treasure ships.

It was on one such expedition to the Azores in 1591 that Sir Richard Grenville, vice-admiral of Lord Thomas Howard's squadron, acted with the rash and heroic bravado that epitomized this kind of warfare. Cut off from the rest of the fleet by a superior Spanish force, the *Revenge*, commanded by Grenville, took on the Spanish single-handed. For fifteen hours the English ship was battered by cannon and musket fire from Spanish galleons until her decks ran with blood and almost every man was dead or wounded.

The *Revenge* had sunk two Spanish ships when called to surrender, but although he was wounded Grenville refused, ordering his master-gunner to blow up the ship rather than give it to the Spanish. At this the surviving members of the crew rebelled. They had been promised excellent terms by the enemy who were impressed by their gallantry and they preferred to trust the enemy to being blown to pieces. Grenville tried to fall on his sword rather than surrender, but his men stopped him and he was taken prisoner. He was treated with the utmost courtesy but legend has it that he broke his wine glass and swallowed the jagged fragments so that the stigma of captivity could not stain his honour. His last words were: 'Here die I, Sir Richard Grenville, with a joyful and quiet mind, for that I have ended my life as a true soldier ought to do that hath fought for his country, queen, religion and honour.'

If this madcap hero could return to his peaceful Cornish estate today he might fume that the old house has been demolished and be pleasantly surprised that his stables have become a traditional farmhouse. If he walked across his old warrens towards the ocean where he spent his last days he might reel in astonishment. On the edge of the Atlantic cliffs rise the strange, vast dishes of a composite signals organization station. A different kind of Elizabethan defender of the realm?

COMPOSITE SIGNALS ORGANIZATION STATION, MORWENSTOW, CORNWALL

'This colour, although not without objection from some quarters on aesthetic grounds has nevertheless received the approval of the Royal Fine Arts Commission and this approval is supported by the Council for the Protection of Rural England . . . thus placing the Post Office in a particularly strong position to justify the choice made.'

THE POST OFFICE ELECTRICAL ENGINEERS' JOURNAL

There are no prizes for guessing what is behind the distinctive red glazing bars of this door: what is missing is the rest of the kiosk. When the public telephone was installed in Guiting Power in Gloucestershire the GPO showed great sensitivity and put it in an existing corner building, using only the red door for instant recognition. If the people of this typical Cotswold village want to use a public telephone they go to the wall, not to a traditional telephone box.

The first telephone kiosks were also rather individual. Known as call stations, these wooden huts, a cross between a sentry box and a rustic garden shed, appeared from 1886. They usually had attendants who waited inside until a customer came along. They placed the call and took the money, then waited outside, whatever the weather, until the caller had finished.

In 1921 standard kiosks called K1 were introduced. They were concrete versions of the wooden boxes with wrought iron ornamentation. They did not last long; in 1924 a competition to design a new kiosk was organized, it was won by the eminent architect Sir Giles Gilbert Scott. Scott's design, K2, was the first familiar red kiosk. The bold colour of this classic design was approved by the Fine Arts Commission, but the box was more popular in London than in country areas, although by 1988 those that remained were listed. Scott also designed a special box to commemorate the Silver Jubilee of George V in 1935. K6 was similar to K2 but had little crowns around the top and different glazing bars on the doors. The Jubilee remained the standard kiosk until 1968.

There were attempts to subvert convention. At Eastbourne telephone kiosks on the sea front were thatched to match the shelters. In places of outstanding natural beauty, boxes were painted battleship-grey, and in the 1970s the Post Office tried to paint all kiosks yellow. In 1984 British Telecom was born and kiosks, canopies and booths in glass, metal and plastic usurped the throne which the red kiosk had held so long. Most of these dignified boxes were removed, dangling at the end of a crane. Some were bought by swingers to turn into garden ornaments, cocktail cabinets and showers, but the rest languished rusting in architectural graveyards and scrapyards.

At least the telephone at Guiting Power has a Jubilee door. It now seems a symbol of continuity, but the building in which it stands, near the village green, represents just how much change has taken place since the cottage was built 200 years ago.

This strangely-shaped corner building was once the home of a blacksmith. There were so many teams of farm horses in the first part of the twentieth century that there was enough work at the forge to keep four men going. By 1952 only one blacksmith remained and when he died the forge died with him. Where bellows roared, and the blacksmith hammered at his anvil while horses waited patiently to be shod, the bus shelter and the public telephone now stand. Behind the window on the first floor is a secret room with a concealed entrance from the cottage next door.

Opposite the telephone box is the green, the hub of village life. The first markets and fairs were held here in about 1330. Badger-baiting, cock-fighting, shin-kicking and morris dancing also went on around the market cross. A war memorial stands on the village green now and the hubbub of past rural life has disappeared. It is so quiet that a cat can take a nap at the foot of the memorial and telephone calls can be made behind the red door in peace.

PUBLIC TELEPHONE, GUITING POWER, GLOUCESTERSHIRE

'It deserves all its fame, for it backs up every claim,
For it beats as it sweeps as it cleans.'

As the tidal wave of London's rush-hour traffic roars through the western suburbs it surges heedlessly past a gleaming iced cake of a building that rises out of the suburban desert like a palace out of wasteland. The building is isolated by the A40 and few pedestrians stop to look closely at it; the rush-hour motorists, hell-bent on Oxford, certainly don't. Which is a pity, because it is worth time, and incites either love or scorn at a second look.

Winged and finned, some of the blocks look as if they might take flight down the runway of the A40. Sheets of glass framed in pale green wrap the corners of the streamlined building, and rows of black, pink and red tiles outline it. An Aztec king's head-dress fans out dramatically over the main door. It is a Thirties science fiction palace touched with the showy confidence of Hollywood. Was it a film mogul's office or Superman-the-Movie's headquarters on Planet Earth? Neither: its glamorous façade was the gift wrapping for something far more mundane – a factory which produced that saviour of the housewife, the vacuum cleaner.

Hoover's model factory at Perivale in West London was opened in 1933 by the Lord Lieutenant of Middlesex, who marked the occasion by switching on a giant 'hoover'. In less than ten years the company progressed from being a four-man operation in a London backstreet to a forceful company selling a thousand machines a week. When the Perivale palace was opened, the managing director called it 'a monument to Hoover Salesmanship'. The salesforce was trained to a feverish pitch, it even had its own song:

'All the dirt, all the grit,
Hoover gets it every bit,
For it beats as it sweeps as it
    cleans.
It deserves all its fame, for it
    backs up every claim,
For it beats as it sweeps as it
    cleans.'

The Second World War did not stop the Hoover production line, the factory switched from producing vacuum cleaners to manufacturing parts for the machinery of war. The 1951 Hoover handbook claimed: 'It is possible that every British aeroplane, tank and armoured vehicle carried at least one Hoover part.' The factory even put on battle dress: it was so near Northolt aerodrome that the white building was draped in camouflage to prevent it from being bombed.

It was never hit and returned to full production after the war. In the 1950s there were over two and a half thousand employees at Perivale, and the canteen (opposite), a separate block built in 1935, was in operation 21 hours a day, 359 days of the year. The catering department produced $1\frac{1}{4}$ million cups of tea; 4,763 kilogrammes of sausages; 1,364 litres of sauce and 375,000 cooked meals a year.

By the 1970s production at Hoover had declined and by 1981 the chairman's report stated that the Perivale site was largely surplus and most work had been moved to Wales. The factory finally closed in 1987 and the last staff to leave hung a notice on the gate saying, 'That's All Folks'.

The building has always provoked comment. During the 1930s the architects, Wallis, Gilbert and Partners, were sometimes accused of 'façadism' in their architecture and their Hoover building did not escape. Comments by the magazine *Architectural Review* so incensed the architects that it is said that one of the partners went to the offices of the magazine with a horsewhip, but luckily the editor had gone out. Nikolaus Pevsner once wrote that the building was '. . . perhaps the most offensive of all the modernist atrocities along this road of typical by-pass factories'.

But if the building has its detractors, it also has champions and in the early 1980s it was listed by the Department of the Environment and protected so that the façade cannot be demolished. The Hoover factory is seen by many Art Deco enthusiasts as a *tour de force* and even that normally cautious band, the surveyors, said in their report after the closure that it was '. . . possibly the most significant arterial road factory of its date, and one of the most attractive'.

Now the Hoover building stands empty and waits for the planners to decide its fate. It may well become a Tesco superstore, but whatever the development the gleaming façade must, by law, be kept. So commuters of the future, fuming in traffic jams on the A40, will be able to pay homage to this splendid white vision of optimism.

HOOVER FACTORY, PERIVALE, MIDDLESEX

'How doth the little busy bee
Improve each shining hour,
And gather honey all the day
From every opening flower!'

ISAAC WATTS

The air here is full of the zooming flight of workaholic bees carrying their plunder back to headquarters. These insects are lucky, they do not have to forage far afield for nectar because the source is on their doorstep. Their hive is set in a prime site at the edge of a field of flowers.

The plants from which the bees collect their lifeline are part of a unique place: the only working lavender farm in England. Standing in the centre of the fields of hazy purple flowers one could be in Provence, not north-west Norfolk, but lavender has become quintessentially English since the Romans brought it to this island from the Mediterranean to scent their baths two thousand years ago. The botanical name for lavender is *Lavandula*, from the latin *lavo*, to wash. No cottage garden is complete without it, the knot gardens of stately homes are often bordered with it, and the discreet perfume of lavender water and soap are symbols of the English gentlewoman. But at Heacham in Norfolk they grow this aromatic and beautiful herb commercially.

Lavender was once so popular that there were several lavender farms in England. It was grown for its flowers which were used in nosegays to keep city smells at bay, or dried and kept with clothes and linen to sweeten them and to keep out moths. It was also grown for its medicinal properties. In the seventeenth century Nicholas Culpeper wrote that it helped to cure 'pains in the head and brain' and that applying lavender water to the temples would help '. . . the tremblings and passions of the heart, and faintings and swoonings . . .'. At the base of each tiny flower is a little sac which contains the oil from which lavender perfume is made and many flowers were grown for this precious commodity. Some of the biggest lavender farms were near London, in places such as Mitcham, but as the capital grew there was more profit in building on the land than in using it to grow lavender and the farms disappeared under the metropolitan sprawl.

But for the enterprise of a Norfolk nurseryman the art of farming lavender in England might have been lost forever. In the early 1930s Linn Chilvers saw the potential of growing lavender commercially. The light, well-drained soil and low rainfall of north-west Norfolk gave ideal conditions for cultivating the plant. After much research and experiment he found that hybrids of *Lavandula vera*, the true lavender, gave the best oils and were resistant to disease. The first field was 2.4 hectares planted with 33,000 cuttings by a workforce of three men and a boy.

Today the 40.5-hectare farm grows about 4,840 lavender bushes to the acre. Six hybrids are used, but these were selected from about a hundred hybrid varieties. Bushes are grown from cuttings to ensure that the original qualities of high yield, excellent perfume and disease resistance are maintained. Lavender growers need patience and foresight as each cutting takes about seven years to mature and the work of producing new plants is constant.

July is harvest time. The rows of lavender bushes stretch purple to the horizon, and the scent of lavender permeates the air. Years ago, when the flowers were harvested by hand, it used to take forty people six weeks to cut the lavender from the bushes with miniature sickles. It was back-breaking work and today the bushes are harvested and pruned by a specially designed machine, the first of its kind in Europe, which can harvest 1.2 to 1.6 hectares a day.

Some of the harvest is dried and used in products such as lavender bags and pot-pourri, but about 101 tonnes is taken to the distillery. Here it is piled into two huge copper stills which each take about 0.254 tonne of flowers, and a smaller one which can hold about 0.127 tonne. The boiler is stoked and once it is roaring, steam passes through the stills for about an hour. The oil in the flowers vapourizes and is cooled in a condenser. The mixture of pure oil and distilled water separates and the oil is drawn off. Each 0.254 tonne of flowers yields about 0.85 litres of pure lavender oil which is used in the making of perfume and perfumed products.

These fields of English flowers, patrolled by bees, butterflies and other nectar-seeking insects, produce lavender for the home market, but this essence of England reaches much further than that. From this corner of Norfolk exports are sent to Australia, Chile, the USA and the remote Norfolk Islands in the Pacific Ocean.

LAVENDER FARM, NEAR HEACHAM, NORFOLK

'. . . deep on his front engraven
Deliberation sat, and public care;
And princely counsel in his face yet shone,
Majestic though in ruin. Sage he stood,
With Atlantean shoulders, fit to bear
The weight of mightiest monarchies; his look
Drew audience and attention still as night
Or summer's noontide air.'

MILTON: *PARADISE LOST*

A weathered and forlorn figure sits in the centre of Crowland in Lincolnshire. Although it still holds its head erect, this worn and lugubrious figure has the air of an exiled king who carries the weight of the world on his shoulders. The disconsolate statue may have a long wait because the path beside it leads to nowhere.

The statue is thought to be Christ the King holding an orb, although local wits have described it as Oliver Cromwell holding a bun. It probably once graced the west front of nearby Crowland Abbey church and was moved to its present spot in about 1720. It has fared better than the abbey, most of which is in ruins. Only the north aisle of the abbey church remains intact and it is used as the parish church.

Crowland Abbey was burnt down three times and shaken by an earthquake before 1190. It was begun by King Ethelbald in 716 and disbanded by Henry VIII at the Dissolution, when the abbot was pensioned off with £133 6s. 8d. for life. King Canute obviously thought more highly of it for records show that he gave the abbey twelve polar bear skins to warm the feet of the priests as they stood at the altar. When Crowland expanded in the eighteenth century, many of the houses were built of stone taken from the monastic site. William Stukeley, the contemporary historian noted that 'you see pieces of it in every house'.

In spite of Henry VIII's harsh treatment, the town of Crowland remained staunchly Royalist during the Civil War. Crowland was on one of the main routes across the Fens, and Cromwell had his eye on it. In 1643 the vicar of Crowland led the townspeople, armed only with 'fennish weapons' such as scythes and pitchforks, against the Parliamentarians. The men of Crowland held out for some time and it took an army under Cromwell's command to suppress them.

Although it is now some distance from the nearest river, the waters of the Fens once poured through Crowland and there is an astonishing piece of evidence to support this fact. In the centre of the town there is a unique triangular bridge of three arches which meet at an angle of 120 degrees. The fourteenth-century arches once spanned three tributaries of the River Welland: but now they span a road junction. The streams have long since been diverted, or ran dry as the Fens were drained, although there is a local legend which says that the waters were sucked down into a whirlpool which still rages underground beneath the bridge.

The bridge was built of Ancaster limestone between 1360 and 1390 and replaced a wooden bridge which existed about one thousand years ago. The fourteenth-century bridge was probably built by the monks of Crowland Abbey as it is also known as Trinity Bridge. It is said that Edward IV came to the bridge by boat on his way to Fotheringhay Castle in Northamptonshire. Another royal visitor was Henry VI, who landed at the bridge when he went to stay with the Abbot of Crowland in 1460. During his visit he gave the town a charter for a market and a fair.

Because it stood at the centre of the town, the bridge became a meeting place. In more recent centuries men used to come to the bridge to be hired as labourers for the day. From the top, where the three arches meet, the town crier used to ring his bell and shout his news.

Now it is a traffic island and the paths over it lead nowhere. Locally it is known

as the Three-Ways-to-Nowhere Bridge.
The stone figure of Christ sits patiently on
one of the arches and watches the passing
traffic.

TRIPLE BRIDGE, CROWLAND, LINCOLNSHIRE

'. . . doth as much exceed Stonehenge in grandeur
as a Cathedral doth an ordinary Parish Church.'

JOHN AUBREY

As light cracks open the clouds a stone sentinel looms on the skyline, a solid contrast to the vaporous sky and fragile tracery of winter trees. It seems to breathe out the enigmatic and ancient spirit of place that embodies the southern heights of England. You cannot walk the sweeping Wiltshire uplands without being haunted by the primeval melancholy of barrows and burials and mysterious stone circles of an age long separated from us.

The standing stone is one of the survivors of the largest stone circle in the world. Avebury Stone Circle was a vast temple, although that description is somewhat simplistic. It was a very important religious centre, built in about 2400 BC. Scanning the OS maps of the area shows that Avebury is surrounded by prehistoric monuments: many barrows, including West Kennet Long Barrow are in the immediate vicinity; as is Silbury, the largest man-made hill in Europe, built six hundred years before Avebury; while Stonehenge is only 27 kilometres to the south. The whole region held a significance for prehistoric people that we can barely begin to imagine today. Avebury was one of its most sacred and powerful sites.

Two words appear at the centre of the Department of the Environment's official plan of Avebury: 'TOILETS' and 'RED LION'. How on earth did a public convenience and public house come to be at the very heart of such a hallowed place? Avebury Stone Circle is so large that it encircles the village of Avebury, which was begun in the Middle Ages and expanded in the seventeenth and eighteenth centuries.

The ancient henge is actually four stone circles enclosed by a massive ditch and bank 1.25 kilometres in circumference. It covers about 11.5 hectares. There were originally ninety-eight stones in the outer circle. Inside this were two circles of about thirty stones each, the fourth circle of twelve stones was inside one of these. Altogether there were about one hundred and eighty monoliths, but only forty-nine have survived. Many were buried in the Middle Ages by nervous locals who deeply mistrusted the stones' pagan origins. One was a barber surgeon whose skeleton was recently excavated; it seems that one of the great stones fell on him as he was helping to bury it.

William Stukeley, the eighteenth-century antiquary, visited and documented the stone circle over several years but had to watch helplessly as villagers plundered the stones for building material and ploughed up the land:

'Thus, this stupendous fabric, which for some thousands of years has braved the continual assaults of the weather, and by the nature of it, when left to itself, like the pyramids of Egypt, would have lasted as long as the globe, has fallen a sacrifice to the wretched ignorance and avarice of a little village, unluckily placed within it.'

When Avebury Stone Circle was constructed, the great stones, some of which weighed more than 60 tonnes, were dragged from the nearby Marlborough Downs, where sarsen, a very hard type of sandstone, is found on the surface. Without the wheel, using ropes, sledges, and man or oxpower, it must have been a mammoth task. The stones were not shaped by human hand, they were used as found. The ditch was dug using tools made from wood, stone or animal bones, and it was originally about 7 metres deep.

The physical construction of such circles was extremely difficult and for centuries was considered wonder enough, but recent research shows that there is more to them than mere circles of stone. The circles at Stonehenge were built in such a way that they could be used as an extremely accurate calculator of the movement of the sun, moon and important stars. To achieve this, the people who built it must have used complex geometry years in advance of Pythagoras, and the builders of other stone circles probably used it too.

The prehistoric peoples who built and used Avebury are separated from us by more than time. They knew the stone circle as a spiritual powerhouse. The knowledge of this power has become diluted over the centuries so that few people today could begin to recognize or experience it. But if you stand among the great sarsen stones as dawn breaks, they seem to emit a power which hangs in the air fusing past millenia with the present, an evocation of a spiritual world long since forgotten.

STONE CIRCLE, AVEBURY, WILTSHIRE

'We bridge across the dark, and bid the helmsman have a care,
The flash that, wheeling inland, wakes his sleeping wife to prayer.
From our vexed eyries, head to gale, we bind in burning chains
The lover from the sea-rim drawn – his love in English lanes.'

RUDYARD KIPLING

The Sole Bay Inn occupies a quiet corner of a peaceful seaside town but the scene belies its past. Many of the pub's customers, supping their Adnam's in the sunshine, are not aware that the town has a lively history, or that the Victorian inn is named after a bloody seventeenth-century sea battle which took place just off the coast.

Today the town is England in genteel aspic, a pretty arrangement of cottages, inns, houses and shops sealed in a gel which has preserved a way of life evocative of the 1920s. People here carry their shopping in baskets, the high street tobacconist keeps a magnificent selection of cigarettes in glass-topped counters, sweets are sold loose from jars and boxes, and every newspaper on display is individually folded. There is nothing mass-produced or packaged about the Suffolk town of Southwold: these are shops as they used to be, where service is important and shopkeepers carry stocks of individual items because some day there might be a call for one of them. It is enchantingly quaint and overrun by tourists in the summer.

During the seventeenth century it was overrun by the Navy. Before the sea eroded the coastline, Sole Bay, formed by Eastern Ness and Dunwich, gave anchorage to the British fleet and Southwold was used as a watering place, and as a land rest for the sick and wounded from ships of the line. Facing the Dutch coast, it saw much action during the wars with Holland and an indecisive and bloody battle, in which the Dutch fleet engaged the French and British, was fought in the bay in 1672. The allies were caught napping and it took four hours to drum sailors, who were enjoying Southwold's inns, back to their ships before the battle could begin. In the mad scramble to man the ships hundreds were left on shore; they were the lucky ones, for many sailors that night of drinking Suffolk ale was their last. For months after the battle corpses were washed ashore and the people of Southwold were paid one shilling for any body that they found and buried.

Men of the sea, especially fishermen, have always been part of the town. At the time of the 'Domesday Book' Southwold paid twenty-five thousand herring to the Abbot of Bury St Edmunds, and by the early sixteenth century it had one of the largest fishing fleets on the east coast and sent many boats to the fishing grounds off Iceland. At the beginning of this century Southwold was used as an overspill harbour for Yarmouth and Lowestoft and sometimes as many as three hundred Scottish fishing vessels crowded the native longshore fishing boats. Just off the market is the Seaman's Reading Room, a Dickensian building where old salts chat, play cards and billiards, and browse among the memorabilia of their way of life. The walls are covered with yellowing photographs labelled with the intriguing names of Southwold fishermen: Sloper, Winkle and Jumbo Hurr, Slummy Ashmanal, Brushy Watson and Bull Smith.

The sea and its dangers have also given Southwold one of its most remarkable landmarks. In a back street of terraced houses, on a garden-sized plot of land, is a lighthouse. Roosting incongruously among the buildings tightly clustered at its sturdy base, it appears to be well inland, as if beached by a receding sea. But its beam, which has a range of 22 nautical miles, is a powerful navigational light with red sectors which warn shipping of shoals to the north, and of the Sizewell bank.

Built in 1890, the round white tower is 31 metres high, the lamp at the top is the equivalent of 243,000 candle power. Until 1938, when it was electrified, the tower was home to a lighthouse keeper, but now it is fully automatic and visited regularly by a local attendant. It is one of the eighty-five lighthouses maintained by Trinity House; of these, just over one-third are automatic and the rest should be by the end of the century.

Approaching Southwold through meadows and cornfields the beautiful church of St Edmund's is the first landmark to stand out. The lighthouse plays hide and seek, an enigma on the skyline, which disappears behind bands of trees, making drivers double-take. At night the beam of this high street lighthouse eerily stabs the dark, lending excitement to this most gentle of seaside towns.

THE LIGHTHOUSE, SOUTHWOLD, SUFFOLK

'From smoke and noise to blooming sweets
Retire a while my fair,
To Twick'n'am's ever blest retreats
And breathe a purer air.'

ANONYMOUS

Swaying sluggishly at its moorings this curious craft looks so exhausted and battered that it might have recently arrived home from a ten-year voyage of discovery. But it has not sailed among icebergs or been nudged by inquisitive whales, nor has it skirmished with pirates in eastern seas: it is a river raft, safely moored in one of the prime locations in the south of England, a tube journey away from the centre of London and a stone's throw from expensive suburban housing.

Heaped with bikes, boxes, crates, drums, tins and buckets and draped with tarpaulins, junk might be a more appropriate term for this floating shanty than raft. But to call it that would not do it justice; it is a defiant original among the sleek glass-fibre launches that ply between the Thames locks on Sunday afternoons, and a curiosity to everyone who passes by, whether afloat or on the tow-path.

It may be a curiosity to the public but to the owner it is home. Launched in London, it was floated up-river on the tide to Twickenham. Once at its mooring it grew, new structures appeared on it and at one point it became a semi-detached residence when a second raft was built and moored in tandem. One night vandals set fire to the original raft and the sound of the exploding oil drum floats reverberated across the river. It was utterly destroyed, but the second raft survived and became a permanent home.

Ducks love it. In the spring the calm water between the raft and the river bank is full of bobbing miniature rafts considerately floated there by the raft owner. Each one is a retreat where ducks can raise their young safe from foxes and drowning – the concrete river bank here is too steep for them to land. Some of the duck rafts have nesting boxes made from wooden crates, others are covered in nesting material and the ducklings splosh busily over and between them. The main raft has little ramps at the side and rear so that the birds can climb out of the water and share the aft deck with the owner. He expertly rescues ducks entangled in discarded fishing line and removes fishing hooks from their mouths. Other birds collect around the raft too: moorhens, coots and Canada geese all use the satellite rafts, although a Canada goose once took up residence in a plastic milk crate on the roof of the main raft. The most exciting birds to nest here are great crested grebe, who rear their speckled chicks beneath the willows and teach them to dive beside the raft.

This idiosyncratic way of life takes place in the centre of one of the most famous views of the River Thames. Seen from the top of Richmond Hill the river below winds away between Petersham Meadows and Marble Hill Park. Several great houses and a palace dot the landscape: Ham House, Marble Hill and Hampton Court. Richmond was a favourite royal retreat for many centuries; Henry VII and Elizabeth I died in Richmond Palace, Richmond Park was created by Charles I and is still a royal park, George II lived in Richmond Lodge in the Old Deer Park. Courtiers and hangers-on built elegant mansions along the river and on the hill, where the rich and famous still choose to live. At Twickenham Alexander Pope lived and wrote, and created his famous grotto. The Duchess of Suffolk entertained him and many other notables of the day at her retreat from court, Marble Hill House. Just near the river steps to Marble Hill

Park the raft swings at its moorings, a drastic contrast to the elegant Palladian house, but a retreat from the city none the less.

THE THAMES, TWICKENHAM, MIDDLESEX

'Life is made up of marble and mud.'

NATHANIEL HAWTHORNE

At Seven Rock Point, west of Lyme Regis, the eroded helix of an ammonite lies exposed to the elements. Once buried in the soft mud of a sea bed, it lay hidden for millions of years until changes in the earth's surface brought it into the open for palaeontologists to study and amateurs to wonder at. Embedded in rock, and rock itself, it is hard to believe that this decorative spiral was once a living creature which swam the prehistoric oceans of the world.

Although ammonites became extinct one hundred million years ago they were not failures as a species, managing to survive for about three hundred million years – humans have so far managed only eighty thousand years. Ammonites were somewhat similar to today's nautilus. There were many different species and their fossils have been found in several continents, in mountain ranges as far apart as the Alps and the Himalayas, and in the soft crumbling cliffs of the Dorset coast.

Jane Austen visited the holiday resort of Lyme Regis in 1804 and set part of her novel *Persuasion* there. The town is still a popular place for a seaside holiday and in the summer the streets can become choked with tourists and their cars. Lyme was popular millions of years ago too, but with species very different from tourists: the sea was rich with marine animals, and elephants, crocodiles, flying reptiles and dinosaurs roamed the area long before human life developed. The Dorset coast is rich with fossil evidence of their existence.

Mary Anning, a fisherman's daughter who was five years old when Jane Austen made her first visit to Lyme, spent much of her childhood exploring the beaches and cliffs in search of fossils. Her father sold them beside the wet fish on his slab. Mary's mother was an active collector of fossils too and she and Mary must often have roamed the coast together. Tradition says that when she was eleven, Mary found a fossil skeleton of a 6.4 metre ichthyosaurus, a marine reptile which lived between 100 and 180 million years ago. It is very likely that she did, but Mary Anning's reputation rests on far more than one popular story.

She developed great skills as a fossil hunter and collector and began to work with the three Philpot sisters who lived in Lyme. The Philpots were also collectors and Mary's skill and knowledge were essential in enriching their collection. They discovered a belemnite (an extinct cuttlefish) sac with the sepia still in it and one of the Philpot sisters drew the specimen using the 170 million-year-old sepia ink from the sac. The Philpots corresponded with some of the great geologists and natural historians of the day, but by 1820 Mary had begun her own correspondence with eminent scientists. In 1824 she described to Professor William Buckland of Oxford University an almost complete skeleton of a plesiosaurus which she had found, and in 1829 Buckland gave a paper to the Geological Association on a pterodactyl which had been collected by Mary. In 1834 Jean Louis Agassiz, the Swiss natural historian went to Lyme to look at the fossil collection.

Until recently Mary Anning was popularly seen through anecdotes as a simple fisherman's daughter who found some dramatic fossils. However, she is emerging as an extremely well-organized, skilful and scientifically-minded woman who supplied the great geologists of the day with invaluable information and examples, and who was a pioneer in the early days of palaeontology.

It is still possible to collect fossils where Mary Anning found hers, but it would be unusual for the tourist to discover anything as exotic as her finds. The most common today are bivalves, ammonites and belemnites which can be picked up from the beaches after rock falls. It is dangerous to climb and hammer at the cliffs in search of fossils because they are so unstable. A safer way is to explore at low tide when the receding sea reveals how life on earth used to be.

Ammonite at Seven Rock Point, near Lyme Regis, Dorset

'Change your dwelling place often,
for the sweetness of life consists in variety.'

ARABIC PROVERB

The cobbled back lanes of this Yorkshire city appear today much as they did in the last century. Standing between yard walls and backs of terraced houses it is easy to imagine the clatter of clogs on cobbles as workers made the morning scramble to get to the mill before the gates clanged shut against them, and those left outside lost a day's pay.

This is Manningham. Buildings which were originally farmhouses still stand at the end of this cobbled lane as proof that it was a rural hamlet until the Industrial Revolution exploded upon Bradford, and Manningham was absorbed by the fastest-growing industrial city of the time. In 1810 the population of Bradford was about 16,000 and there were 5 power mills, by 1841 there were 120 mills and the population was 66,718, by 1851 it had increased to 103,786. Huge textile mills were built in Manningham in the second half of the nineteenth century. They produced silk and velvet as well as wool. The mill owners built and owned row upon row of terraced houses which they let to their workers. From birth to death, the mill workers were virtually owned by the proprietors.

Along the back lanes of the terraced houses cast-iron gratings are set into the walls. These decorative metal plates are remnants of domestic life decades ago. What their exact purpose was is now a matter of speculation, but it is thought that they were originally ventilation covers for the outside privy, or midden as it is still called locally. The cobbled lanes were made fairly wide to give the night soil cart access to the midden on the back wall of each yard. Most of the middens have now gone, and the ventilation gratings are sometimes used as coal holes, which, some argue, was their original purpose.

The area has changed in other ways. During the 1950s the mill owners re-equipped their mills and to minimize the expense they ran their new machines twenty-four hours a day. Women were the traditional workforce in the mills but with family obligations they did not want to work on the night shifts, so they gradually found different work. Since they no longer needed to live near the mill they and their families began to move out to new estates. The proprietors began to look for a new workforce for the textile industry and they found it in Asia, mostly in Pakistan, where they recruited men to work the night shifts. During the 1960s they were joined by their families and there are now third-generation Bradford-born Asians.

The Muslim population of Bradford is estimated to be about seventy-five thousand and there are twenty-five mosques to lead their spiritual, moral and cultural life. Most of these are house-conversions, but there is one purpose-built mosque and three more are being built. In Manningham some Muslims use a large tent as a temporary mosque while Bradford's largest mosque so far is being built near by. When it is finished the Hanafia Mosque in Manningham will have enough space for 750 men and 250 women to pray beneath its gold-coloured dome; the prayer hall will be convertible for use as classrooms for up to 300 children. It will be a community centre as well as a mosque.

The back lanes of Manningham no longer have traditional alley smells. With a ninety per cent Asian population, far more exotic scents, such as spices, waft in the air. Just the other side of these dour walls the streets are vibrant with the village life of Pakistan. And the sound of the faithful being called to prayer is far more likely than the clatter of clogs on the cobbles.

HANAFIA MOSQUE, MANNINGHAM, BRADFORD

'I will but look upon the hedge and follow you.'

SHAKESPEARE: *THE WINTER'S TALE*

The sinuous laurel curves of a hedge maze are coiled on the side of a valley like a huge green python. Such a creature would not be out of place here at Glendurgan Gardens as it is a Cornish Eden. Crammed with exotic species which flourish in the mild climate, the garden tumbles down to the Helford River in green profusion, a paradise of plants from all over the world.

Planting at Glendurgan was begun in the 1820s and '30s by Alfred Fox, a shipping agent. In those days ships arrived at Falmouth from the Americas, Africa, India, China, Australia and New Zealand, and the Fox family commissioned travellers to bring plants to their Cornish home. Alfred Fox planted a richly varied collection which was added to by his descendants. It includes tulip trees, rhododendrons, bamboos, tree ferns, cypresses from Japan, North America and Mexico, an Atlas Mountain Cedar, a Monterey Pine, a Californian Redwood, magnolias, Chusan Palms and many other rare plants. In the mossy dampness ferns and bog plants such as kingcups flourish and in the spring the valley is strewn with primroses, Chinese primulas and bluebells.

The maze was planted in 1833 by Alfred Fox on the steepest slope of the valley. Mazes were popular at the time but the one at Glendurgan is unusual for its coiling informality, most mazes of the period being symmetrical in design. Glendurgan maze was the forerunner of a Victorian revival of maze building. About eighty were planted but few survive, even Prince Albert's maze disappeared under the Science Museum when it was built.

There were many mazes in England before the nineteenth-century revival, but most have fallen into disrepair. Their history is ancient and mysterious. The earliest are not hedge mazes at all but are cut into the turf. The turf maze at Brandsby in North Yorkshire is cut in a labyrinth design which originated in Ancient Crete – the home of the dreadful Minotaur who lived in a labyrinth. It is impossible to say how a design from Knossos, based on concentric circles came to be cut in English turf, but the Brandsby maze may date back to the Viking occupation, as similar designs are found in Scandinavia. Such early mazes were pagan in origin and are thought to have been used for pagan rituals and dances; the

design of circles probably symbolized the cycle of life, death and rebirth. Only four survive intact, but there are two small Bronze Age labyrinths of similar design carved into rock at Tintagel in Cornwall.

During the Middle Ages many more turf mazes were cut using a Christian form of the pagan design which was quartered by a cross. It is thought that these mazes were used for painful penance by monks who crawled the paths on their knees. A similar design is found in Chartres Cathedral where a mosaic maze, 12.2 metres across, is set into the floor. Pagan designs were happily adopted and adapted and used for symbolic pilgrimages.

By Shakespeare's time the numerous turf mazes in England had fallen into disuse. Many were overgrown 'for lack of tread', and the Elizabethans preferred to concentrate on their knot gardens, from which the hedge maze developed later. John Aubrey, writing in the 1680s, gives one of the very few eye-witness accounts of surviving mazes which were, he wrote, '. . . much used by the young people on Holydaies and by ye School-boies'.

The famous maze at Hampton Court is

the oldest surviving hedge maze in England. It was replanted with yews in 1690 so must have existed before that. Hedge mazes were grown for pleasure and entertainment, unlike turf mazes they were puzzles containing a choice of paths and dead ends. Many hedge mazes were destroyed or left to go wild during the two World Wars, but the 1970s and '80s saw a revival of interest in both path and hedge mazes. New mazes were designed, built and planted – Chatsworth House in Derbyshire being one of the first sites to have a new maze.

But the old survives in tranquillity at Glendurgan, surrounded by a verdant and beautiful garden. The maze is far from retirement as the gardens belong to the National Trust and its paths are well trodden by visitors who enjoy the challenge of this organic puzzle.

THE MAZE, GLENDURGAN GARDENS, HELFORD RIVER, CORNWALL

'*A woman of masculine understanding and conduct,
proud, furious, selfish and unfeeling.
She was a builder, a buyer and seller of estates, a money lender,
a farmer and a merchant of lead, coals and timber. . . .*'

EDMUND LODGE

Blazoned across the skyline the initials 'ES' are visible for miles. They are repeated fifteen times across the roof turrets, proclaiming power, wealth and an indestructible ego. The initials are those of Elizabeth, Countess of Shrewsbury, and they adorn the house which she built between 1590 and 1597. It is hard to think of another house in England which is so inextricably linked with a personality. And what a personality: Bess of Hardwick was a formidable woman and Hardwick Hall in Derbyshire still testifies the fact nearly four hundred years after her death.

Born in 1527 to a family of minor gentry of Hardwick in Derbyshire, Bess married four times, making sure that each marriage took her up the social and financial scale. Her last marriage, in 1567, was to the Earl of Shrewsbury, head of one of the richest, oldest, and most powerful families in the country. After seventeen years the marriage broke down amid public scandal and scrutiny. Undaunted, Bess set about creating her own power base. She bought her birthplace at Hardwick from her debt-ridden brother and spent extravagant sums

replacing the existing house with another, now known as Hardwick Old Hall. But it did not satisfy her and when her estranged husband died in 1590, leaving Bess one of the richest people in England, she decided to build a new house next to the old. Visitors to Hardwick today are surprised to see two great houses so close together, although the Old Hall is now a ruin.

The foundations were laid while Bess lived in and completed the Old Hall. Over the next seven years the New Hall rose in the shadow of the Old. It is a magnificent example of a great Elizabethan house. Bess incorporated in it all the architectural features which the Elizabethans held most dear and it is an uncompromising symbol of wealth and power.

For a start it is symmetrical and the Elizabethans had a great love of symmetry. It was planned as a whole and the interior and exterior are a harmonious marriage. To achieve such symmetry and incorporate the required number and size of rooms, the designer had to cheat: some of the windows are false and have chimneys behind them, others which give the external impression of lighting one storey, actually rise through four storeys

inside the house. Hardwick's great windows are famous and gave rise to the little rhyme, 'Hardwick Hall, more glass than wall'. Glass was an Elizabethan status symbol and the expanses of glass at Hardwick were Bess's proclamation of her material success, even though they made the house extremely cold in winter.

Bess was about sixty-three when the house was begun. At a time when the average life expectancy at birth was probably about twenty-two or twenty-three and only a fifth of the population survived into their seventies it was a considerable age to begin such a project, but Bess's ambition for herself and her family was undiminished. She threw herself into planning every detail of the house. Her aim was to impress, and to that end she had the height of the turrets raised as they were built and she placed the magnificent state rooms on the second floor, rather than the first which was more usual in great houses of the time.

The building materials were hers: stone came from just down the hill, timber from Bess's woods, glass from her glassworks at Wingfield, Blackstone from her Derbyshire quarries, iron from her iron works, lead from her lead workings and alabaster from nearby Creswell. An army of workmen and craftsmen were employed to work on the house. Some of them, such as John Ballechouse, the painter responsible for the painted frieze in the Long Gallery, were loyal to this fierce woman for many years.

The household was dominated by women. Bess's highest paid servant was a gentlewoman called Mrs Digby who earned three times more than her husband who was also a member of the household. One of Hardwick's greatest treasures is its collection of embroideries, some of which were worked by Bess and her gentlewomen. The Countess employed several embroiderers on her permanent staff, some of whom were men, but the embroideries often feature women. Among them are wall hangings depicting Bess's favourite heroines.

But this sixteenth-century tycoon decorated the entrance to her withdrawing room with a soldier's head surmounted by a flaming grenade. One can only speculate what mincemeat she would have made of the twentieth-century planners who built the M1 across the bottom of her garden.

HARDWICK HALL, DERBYSHIRE

'. . . dire portents appeared . . . and sorely frightened the people . . .
immense whirlwinds and flashes of lightning, and fiery dragons were seen
flying in the air. A great famine immediately followed . . . and a little after . . .
the ravages of the heathen men miserably destroyed God's church . . . with
plunder and slaughter.'

THE ANGLO-SAXON CHRONICLE

Here is a landscape whose sweeping moorland and coastline breathes life into the Dark Ages. An ancient land of contrasts, once raw with strife and bloodshed, Northumbria was also the cradle of Christianity. Its rocky islands were the retreat of ascetic monks and where sea-borne Norse warriors beached their dragon-prowed longships, intent on murderous plunder.

Holy Island, just off the Northumbrian coast, is an orderly and peaceful place, visited for its rich variety of wildlife, its ruined priory and its National Trust castle, but its early history was significant and turbulent. This tiny island, only 9.7 kilometres in circumference, was the base from which not one, but two founding saints of English Christianity, St Aidan and St Cuthbert set about reconverting the relapsed Anglo-Saxons with missionary zeal.

Aidan founded a monastery on the island, which was then called Lindisfarne, in about 635. His disciples travelled throughout the country, tramping the moors and preaching in the loneliest hill huts. Aidan, the first Bishop of Lindisfarne was buried beside the high altar. In 664 Cuthbert joined the religious community on the island and it

was probably during his bishopric that the exquisite Lindisfarne Gospels were written on vellum made from the skins of more than one thousand calves. Cuthbert preferred to live on the Farne Islands just to the south, but after his death in 687 his body was brought back to Lindisfarne.

Neither of these charismatic saints had to face the ordeal of the monks who continued their mission. The Vikings leapt on to the rocky shore of Lindisfarne on 8 June 793, slaughtered the monks and plundered and destroyed the church. It was the first known Viking raid on England and heralded the centuries of terror which followed. The monks of Lindisfarne struggled to continue their work but in 875 they fled from the pagan invaders, carrying the precious relics of St Aidan and St Cuthbert and the Lindisfarne Gospels, and never returned to the island.

Lindisfarne was uninhabited for two centuries until 1093 when a Benedictine order from Durham founded a priory there. From then on the island was given the new name of Holy Island. The priory was abandoned at the Dissolution in 1537, but its atmospheric ruins remain.

Holy Island changed from a spiritual to a

military centre in the sixteenth century. Stone from the abandoned priory was used to build the castle between 1549 and 1550. The Scots were harrying the border and the island's natural harbour was a convenient place to land English troops. The castle was built to protect it. But the 'dainte little fort' never fired a shot in action; its fate was far more peaceful.

'Have got Lindisfarne.' read a telegram sent to the architect Edwin Lutyens in 1902. The sender, Edward Hudson, founder of *Country Life* magazine, had scaled the walls of the abandoned castle while exploring Northumbria and saw the potential of the romantic fortress set on Beblowe Crag. Hudson's dream was to turn the inside into a habitable holiday home and he employed the best country house architect of the day to realize it.

The shape of the castle harmonizes with its rock so perfectly that they seem welded together. In fact, Lutyens altered the silhouette of the fort by rounding its edges and removing the crenellation. Inside he created an exciting interior, retaining all the atmosphere of the castle with pillars, arches, winding staircases and vaulted rooms with great fireplaces. Some of the rooms have mesmerizing views of the island or the sea. Not all the visitors were as enchanted as the owner. Lutyens' wife complained of the cold and the smoke from the fires and candles – there was no electricity. Lytton Strachey, the historian, wrote that the castle was 'very dark, with nowhere to sit, and nothing but stone under, over and round you, which produces a distressing effect'.

The island has seen much, from the dire portents recorded in the Anglo-Saxon Chronicle to a holiday haven, frequented by ornithologists and tourists. But it holds its atmosphere and making the crossing to it along the causeway at low tide brings excitement and expectation as the island looms nearer.

LINDISFARNE CASTLE, HOLY ISLAND, NORTHUMBERLAND

'I wonder if we could contrive . . . some magnificent myth
that would in itself carry conviction to our whole community.'

PLATO

Perched in their eyrie high above the River Mersey are two of the most enigmatic creatures in England. Hawk-eyed and fiercely beaked they glare out across the city whose name they share. The sculptured birds that crown the Royal Liver Building are a very real presence, but the Liver Bird is one of Liverpool's great myths.

Stories of its origin are as numerous as ferries across the Mersey. Some say that it rose phoenix-like out of the liver pool, others that it is either an eagle or a cormorant and that it carries a sprig of broom, or a piece of lyver seaweed in its beak. What is certain is that the Liver Bird is a modern, rather than an ancient, myth, and that it was born of confusion.

The eagle was the symbol of King John, who granted the first charter to Liverpool in 1207, and for centuries a bird like an eagle was incorporated in Liverpool's seal. By the seventeenth century Liverpool had forgotten the eagle and had begun to use the cormorant as its symbol. The bird on the original seal is indistinct but it may have been a cormorant because the birds were common in the Mersey estuary. The cormorant has been the official emblem of the city since 1797. Over the years popular myth combined the eagle and the cormorant to produce a hybrid – the fabulous Liver Bird. When the Royal Liver Building was so grandiosely topped with two Liver Birds, part eagle, part cormorant in 1911, the myth was fixed forever in Liverpool's legends.

Liverpool's waterfront is graced by some elegant buildings, the most impressive being the Royal Liver Building. Built to house the Royal Liver Friendly Society, it took three years to complete and was opened on 19 July 1911. The building was constructed on the then new and revolutionary Hennebique Principle in which the inner structure, rather than the outer walls, supports the 141,500 cubic metres of the building. The reinforced concrete skeleton is wrapped with about 25,400 tonnes of granite which clad the outer walls and add to the dramatic impact of this huge office block.

From the ground to the top of the Liver Birds, the building is 98 metres high. To give some idea of the scale, the bronze birds are 5.5 metres high, with a wingspan of 3.7 metres, and each head alone is 1.06 metres long. They were made by the Bromsgrove Guild between 1908 and 1911, and are supported by steel girders and wires and have so far withstood the winds that race down the estuary. So has the famous clock, whose four opal glass faces were constructed to withstand a wind pressure of 1.7 tonnes per square centimetre. The clock is huge: each face is 7.6 metres in diameter, each copper minute hand is 4.3 metres long. It was the largest electrically-operated clock in the United Kingdom when it was installed in 1911, and is larger than the clock on the tower which houses Big Ben at Westminster.

On the pier near the Liver Building stands a memorial. It was originally intended for the engineers who died when the *Titanic* sank in April 1912, but as the public subscription grew the people of Liverpool decided to broaden the dedication and the final inscription reads: 'In honour of all heroes of the marine engine room.'

Liverpool has its share of heroes, myths and legends, and new ones are added by the rich Liverpudlian sense of humour, which says that if an unmarried pregnant girl passes by the Liver Birds will flap their bronze wings. With their bird's eye view of the city, the mythological creatures must see much but they say little.

THE ROYAL LIVER BUILDING, LIVERPOOL

'Was the aim frustrated by force or guile,
When giants scooped from out the rocky ground,
Tier under tier, this semicirque profound?'

WILLIAM WORDSWORTH

In the swirling warmth of a prehistoric shallow tropical sea countless creatures lived and died. Standing on the bare, windswept limestone of the Yorkshire Dales it is hard to imagine that the whole of western Yorkshire was once covered by such a sea and that the rock beneath your feet was created by billions of microscopic sea creatures.

Obviously this is not recent history, the limestone has taken millennia to form. When the area was sea, 330 million years ago, billions of animals lived and died in it. Their shell-like skeletons sank slowly through the warm water to the sea bed and layer upon layer formed limestone. It is hard to grasp the fact that the remnants of minute creatures could form the basis of such dramatic scenery. They did not do it alone of course, other rock layers formed on top of the original limestone, and when the sea retreated massive earth movements lifted, folded and cracked the earth's surface. After that it was left to ice and water to carve the landscape.

Ice, up to a kilometre thick in places, covered the rock during different periods of the Ice Age. It carved the scars, crags, cliffs and wide, steep-sided valleys that are

the landscape of the Yorkshire Dales. When the ice finally retreated, the limestone, scoured clean by the action of glaciers, was left to the mercy of wind and rain.

The wild limestone scenery of the Dales has attracted many visitors, including writers, poets and artists. J.M.W. Turner painted here for part of every summer between 1808 and 1825. Daniel Defoe came earlier and wrote of the '. . . high mountains which had a terrible aspect . . .'. Wordsworth travelled through on his honeymoon and Ruskin was a frequent visitor. Charles Kingsley, author of *The Water Babies*, stayed at Malham Tarn House and set his novel in the rocky landscape of Malham Tarn and Malhamdale.

Sometimes the bald white rock of the limestone plateau gives the landscape a lunar aspect. Huge slabs of rock, separated by deep crevices, stretch out as bare and gleaming as a new pavement, which is why these earthly moonscapes came to be called limestone pavements. Over thousands of centuries rainwater has eaten into the exposed limestone and etched runnels across it, which have gradually

become wider and deeper rifts known as 'grikes'. They can be up to 0.3 metres wide and can be as much as 3.6 metres deep. The blocks of limestone between are called 'clints'. Walking on the limestone pavements needs extreme care – trap your leg in a grike and it can snap like a carrot.

One of the most famous limestone pavements in the Dales is that above Malham Cove. Here there are many clints, and the grikes are deeply etched. At first glance the pavement looks barren, but here and there shade-loving plants such as ferns grow in the grikes. The pavement is in a spectacular position on the edge of the cliffs of Malham Cove. From it the view down Malhamdale is unforgettable. As is the cove.

Below, a beck flows from beneath the cove and plunges down the dale. Water played a major part in shaping the cove. The Ice Age meltwaters, unable to sink into caverns and caves beneath the ground because they were frozen solid, escaped by cascading over the edge of the cliff in a breathtaking waterfall which must have been as large as Niagara Falls. It cut the cliff into the horseshoe shape seen today. Once the ice had melted, water was able to sink into the myriad passages, caves and holes that puncture limestone, and the waterfall ceased.

It is a huge bite out of the landscape, as if some monolithic beast has tried out its dentures on the porous rock. The sheer cliffs rise to nearly 77 metres in a natural amphitheatre of a greenish-white. It has been well known to tourists for two hundred years but even they cannot detract from its splendour. Above it, rock-strewn fields stretch to the skyline bisected by sinuous ribbons of stone wall, while the Pennine Way climbs its western flank.

MALHAM COVE, MALHAM, YORKSHIRE

Brayer, damsel, fan gallery,
horse, quant, shore,
smutter, spider, spout,
sweep, wallower, wormwheel.

The quaint words on the previous page are an exercise in the naming of parts. They are all words which describe different parts of a windmill, Polegate Windmill in Sussex. The 'damsel' is part of the mechanism that keeps the corn moving down through the mill towards the millstones. It was apparently given its name because it makes the most noise in the mill, although it must take an experienced ear to hear it over the cacophony of grunting and rattling that fills and shakes a windmill when it is hard at work.

Polegate was last worked by wind in 1943, and was one of the last windmills to use wind power in England. There were about ten thousand working windmills in England at one time, but by 1919 steam and electricity had taken over as sources of power and there were only about three hundred and fifty left. By 1946 the number had reduced to fifty. Since then several have been saved and have either been, or are in the process of being, restored. Only a handful are in full working order and Polegate is still being renovated.

Built in 1817, Polegate Windmill is a tower mill and used wind power to grind corn for 129 years. It is now owned by the Eastbourne Civic Society which bought it in 1965 and has been raising money and overseeing its restoration since then. It is a long task, as an experienced millwright is needed for the work and many of the parts must be specially made from particular kinds of wood.

The tower is 14.3 metres high and built of red brick. Windows and doors are built in a spiral around the windmill. In early tower mills, windows were built one above the other but this sometimes weakened the structure and caused the tower to crack. At the top of the Polegate tower is a dome cap, 2.13 metres high, topped with an acorn finial. The entire cap turns, rather like a giant pepper mill, so that the sails can be brought into the wind. At right angles to the sails, and on the opposite side of the cap, is a fantail which keeps the sails turned into the wind. Before Edmund Lee invented the fantail in 1745, the cap and sails had to be turned by the miller or his assistant. Turning a huge piece of machinery in a strong wind must have been back-breaking work.

Polegate's sails, or sweeps as they are called in Sussex, are 19.5 metres long. Each has a twist, rather like a propeller, so that they can make the most of the wind. In addition each sweep has shutters, like the louvres on a venetian blind, which can be closed in a breeze, or opened to spill some of the wind if it strengthens. This system, called the spring sail, was invented in 1772 by a millwright called Andrew Meikle. Polegate's sweeps are patent sails, which means that the shutters on all four sweeps can be controlled at the same time.

The earliest recorded windmill in England was working in 1185. From then until the eighteenth century the sails were wooden lattices to which canvas was lashed. When the wind strengthened the miller had to stop the sails and unlash the canvas on each one, a desperate and dangerous job in a high wind. If the sails ran uncontrolled, the mill could destroy itself, but if the miller applied the brakes too hard in a strong wind, the heat of friction could set the whole mill on fire. The miller had to keep corn running to the millstones and pray that it would not run out before the wind subsided.

Large tower mills might have as many as eight pairs of millstones. Polegate has three, each of which is 1.3 metres in diameter. One pair is of Derbyshire Peak stone and used for course grinding, such as animal food. The other two are of French Burr and used for grinding corn into flour. Each stone is 'dressed' or grooved to help with the grinding process. The grooves can wear out very quickly and some millstones had to be 'dressed' or re-cut every two or three days. At Polegate the stones were usually dressed every few weeks.

When the last miller of Polegate, Albert Ovenden, died in 1973, the sails were set in the millers' distress sign – a St George's Cross. They are still in that position today, perhaps in protest at the sea of houses which has crept, like an incoming tide, to the foot of its tower. But Polegate Windmill is fortunate: it has been saved; and now that wind as an alternative source of power is becoming increasingly viable and essential, the sweeps of windmills like Polegate may once more turn.

TOWER MILL, POLEGATE, SUSSEX

'When Orpheus tuned his lyre, he played so well,
The rocks and trees came down, the strain to greet,
But thou, Mancunium, with a mightier spell,
Hast drawn great Neptune to thy lordly feet.'

W. BLAKE ATKINSON

Chugging along the Bridgewater Canal near Manchester boats come to Barton Aqueduct. At first glance it appears an ordinary aqueduct carrying the Bridgewater Canal over the Manchester Ship Canal, the only strange thing about it being the red gantry which surrounds it. The canal passes beneath the gantry an innocent and continuous strip of water, giving no clue that it is actually flowing across a miracle of nineteenth-century engineering.

Barton Aqueduct moves. The whole structure is a huge metal trough which can be swung aside, full of water, to allow ships to pass along the Manchester Ship Canal. It seemed a wild idea when it was first thought of: the trough is 71.3 metres long, 2.1 metres deep, 5.5 metres wide and weighs about 1,524 tonnes, including 813 tonnes of water. Some thought that the engineer who designed it had overstretched his imagination. However, Sir Edward Leader Williams proved the sceptics wrong, and such was the perfection of his design that the aqueduct works as efficiently today as it did when it was opened in 1893.

Originally there was a three-arched stone aqueduct where the swing aqueduct now stands. Brindley's aqueduct of 1761 carried the Bridgewater Canal over the River Irwell. In its day it was just as innovative as Leader Williams's and met with even more incredulity. Nothing like it had been seen in England before; it was called 'the greatest artificial curiosity in the world'. Brindley's historic aqueduct lasted for 130 years but was taken down during the construction of the Manchester Ship Canal which swallowed up the River Irwell. Large ships using the new waterway could not pass under it and Leader Williams was faced with the problem of designing an aqueduct which could accommodate them. Barton Aqueduct was the result.

The mechanism which operates the aqueduct is a brilliant piece of hydraulic engineering. The aqueduct is usually kept in alignment with the Bridgewater Canal. When a ship approaches on the Manchester Ship Canal, the water in the Bridgewater Canal is sealed off at both ends of the aqueduct with hydraulically operated metal gates. Similar gates seal the water in the aqueduct, which is kept watertight by huge rubber-faced wedges,

each weighing 12.2 tonnes. The huge trough is pivoted on an island in the centre of the Ship Canal. It revolves on roller bearings and is turned by hydraulic machinery operated from a tower on the island. As it moves, a central hydraulic press takes the great weight off the rollers.

Watching Barton Aqueduct swing open is memorable. Any piece of machinery that size ought to make an incredible noise, but the aqueduct swings to its island rest in the centre of the Ship Canal in eerie silence. It is like a huge piece of Meccano in a model landscape. As it swings, the water in the trough is strangely still. When it comes to a standstill a swell of water rolls from one end of the trough to the other. Moving the aqueduct takes about two minutes, although the complete operation takes about twenty minutes. The men who operate the machinery take great pride in their unique charge, and the machinery house is full of gleaming brass wheels and buttons. They tell of days when the Manchester Ship Canal was far busier than it is now and there were teams of smartly uniformed men in charge of the aqueduct.

The meeting point of the Bridgewater

Canal and the Manchester Ship Canal makes Barton Aqueduct an historic place. The engineering problems tackled and solved during the building of both canals were of great significance to the future of waterways and industrialization. The Bridgewater Canal was not the first canal to be built in England but the daring of its owner and of its engineer showed what could be done and triggered the great age of canal building in Britain. The Manchester Ship Canal, built 130 years later, also broke new ground in engineering – in both cases the seemingly impossible was achieved.

English waterways have seen great days, have fallen into decline, and have seen a revival of interest, mostly for recreation. Although traffic on the Bridgewater Canal and the Manchester Ship Canal has decreased drastically, neither has stopped working. With increasing congestion on the roads some experts believe that the future of transport in England rests on the canals, so it is possible that Barton Aqueduct will be swinging well into the next century.

BARTON AQUEDUCT: THE BRIDGEWATER CANAL MEETS THE MANCHESTER SHIP CANAL

'Heaven and earth shall pass away,
but my words shall not pass away.'

ST MATTHEW 24: 35

Carved on tablets of stone among the boulders strewn around the rocky summit of a hill are some almost indecipherable words. A closer look reveals that that they are the Ten Commandments. This is not Mount Sinai but a bleak hilltop in Devon where the severe weather has eroded the words, although they are carved in granite.

The biblical verses were cut at the whim of the local lord of the manor. The Whitley family lived at Buckland Court and Mr Whitley commissioned the carving to celebrate the defeat in the House of Commons of the Revised Prayer Book Measure in 1927. He chose two slabs of moorstone – the local name for surface granite – near the top of Buckland Beacon on Dartmoor and set a stonemason, Mr A.W. Clements, to work in the winter of 1928–9.

Moses may have had a hard time when he collected the originals at the top of Mount Sinai, but life was not that easy for Mr Clements either. Buckland Beacon is 390.7 metres, quite high enough to make a man breathless after the climb. Mr Clements is said to have slept in a barn near the tor for the two or more months

that he worked on the carvings, but must have made the climb to the top every working day. Mr Whitley, who nicknamed the stonemason 'Moses', provided him with a loaf of bread a week, which hardly seems manna from heaven.

Buckland Beacon is one of southern Dartmoor's best-known tors. There are about two hundred tors on Dartmoor, ranging in size from small groups of boulders to towering rock piles. An inscription at the top of Buckland Beacon records that a fire was lit there to celebrate George V's Silver Jubilee.

Dartmoor's foundation is granite, which, although it is a hard rock, has weak planes, and these have been eroded, leaving the dramatic outcrops of rock that are the tors. Some of them have been weathered into grotesque shapes which loom over the moors. The groups of boulders strewn on the slopes below the outcrops are known as 'clitters'. Granite from Dartmoor was used to make one of London's most famous landmarks, Nelson's Column in Trafalgar Square.

Several of the summits on Dartmoor are over 580 metres and two are over

610 metres, which means that some of the tors are on very high ground. Yet most are accessible and the views from the top are a breathtaking reward for the scramble to the summit. The highest tor on the moor is High Willhays which reaches 621 metres. Vixen Tor is on low ground, but the outcrop of rock is the tallest on the moor, reaching 30.5 metres above the ground. Hay Tor (454.5 metres) is the most visited on Dartmoor and has magnificent views as far as the English Channel. Hound Tor is said to have been haunted by a phantom hound from Hell which inspired Conan Doyle to write his Sherlock Holmes thriller, *The Hound of the Baskervilles*.

Most of Dartmoor was designated a national park in 1951. The importance of conserving the moor was realized as early as 1883 when the Dartmoor Preservation Society was founded. It was set up originally to protect rights of way and ancient sites but is now a pressure group to preserve the whole of England's 'last great southern wilderness'. Within the park lie 945 square kilometres of sponge-like black peat, moorland, coombs (valleys), treacherous mires, ancient woodland, mountains, and a few towns and villages – and the tors.

Buffeted by the wind and the deluging rain the fantastic shapes of the tors can bring the atmosphere of the Old Testament to the moor. Perhaps this biblical landscape inspired the carving of the Ten Commandments on Buckland Beacon, but the view from the summit was probably inspiration enough.

THE TEN COMMANDMENTS STONE, BUCKLAND BEACON, DARTMOOR, DEVON

Carnation, Lavender, Wallflower,
Aniseed, Cinnamon, Peppermint,
Violet, English Rose, Jasmine,
Almond, Heliotrope, Attar of Roses,
Lemon, Raspberry, Apricot,
Mandarin, Sandalwood, Patchouli,
Pine Forest, Eucalyptus, Rosemary.

As huge cogs turn, oak pestles spin in iron mortars, grumbling as they grind. The noise is thunderous. This robust and functional machinery begins a process which ends with such delicate scents as carnation, lavender, rose, geranium, peppermint, wallflower and bergamot.

The machinery is antique. It was originally used in the manufacture of gunpowder, so it was already second-hand when it was installed for its present purpose in 1792. It has been used ever since, and is said to be the oldest machinery in daily use in England, producing what Alexander Pope called 'pungent grains of titillating dust' – snuff.

Samuel Gawith and Co. Ltd has been making snuff since 1792. At present it produces about 13,600 kilograms of snuff a year using these grand old pestles and mortars in its Kendal factory. (It also uses modern machinery for finely-powdered snuffs.) Top quality tobacco leaf is ground to a powder, and then natural scents are added in various combinations to make the hundreds of different blends of snuff which the company produces. The recipes are highly secret and are kept locked away:

only three people have access to them. It takes a natural aptitude and years of experience to become a snuff blender expert in the art of blending the raw materials into the right texture, colour and aroma.

Snuff blenders may take snuff but they are not frequent users as they have to preserve their finely developed ability to differentiate between the various scents in a blend. Some snuffs may have as many as twenty or thirty different scents in them; all are natural essences. The company makes special orders, ranging from coffee to cologne, for individual customers, and will attempt any blend – 'even baked bean if requested'.

Adventurers on Columbus's second voyage of 1493–6 saw American Indians sniffing strange powder, tried it, and brought the custom back to Europe. By the sixteenth century snuff had become extremely popular in France and Spain. No one knows exactly when snuff arrived in England but it was certainly in use during the reign of Elizabeth I. Charles II took it and so did Queen Anne. During her reign taking snuff was almost more popular than smoking a pipe. By the early

eighteenth century there were over four hundred snuff shops in London alone. Princess Charlotte, wife of George III, took so much that she was nicknamed 'Snuffy Charlotte'. Fashionable ladies were never without their snuff boxes: a certain Margaret Thompson even asked to be buried in one. She requested that her coffin be filled with snuff and 'handkerchiefs a plenty', such was her love of the powdered tobacco leaf. But Dr Johnson shunned the snuff box, preferring to fill the pockets of his vast coat with loose snuff. Pope, Swift, Dryden, Garrick, Congreve and Gibbon all took snuff and Samuel Gawith used to supply Marie Lloyd, the music-hall entertainer.

Apart from the social pleasures of taking it, snuff has long been advocated as a remedy for many ailments. In 1610 Gardiner wrote that it

'. . . must needes doe good where the brain is repleat with many vapours, for those that have a lethargy, or vertiging, in all long griefes, paines and aches of the head, in continuall senselesses, or benumming of the braine, and for a hicket that proceedeth of repletion'.

People today use medicated snuffs to relieve catarrh and hayfever, to clear the sinuses, and to prevent coughs and colds. Unlike other tobacco products in England, snuff does not have to carry a health warning.

The unique machinery at Samuel Gawith produces an average of 136 kilograms of snuff a day which is exported all over the world, and snuff is still popular in England. People from all walks of life, including doctors, MPs and clergy enjoy the 'titillating dust'. Miners take it too because they cannot smoke underground. It seems that, like these impressive eighteenth-century pestles and mortars, the appeal of snuff has an enduring quality.

SAMUEL GAWITH'S SNUFF MILL, KENDAL, CUMBRIA

'*Time and tide wait for no man.*'

PROVERB

Towards the end of its journey across northern England that enormous plate of rock the Great Whin Sill rears up in a coastal crag before it makes its final plunge into the cold waters of the North Sea. Gripping the crag is England's most dramatic sea castle, the grand finale to a region freely punctuated with pele towers, castles and all manner of fortifications.

Bamburgh Castle has stood on its Northumbrian rock for almost nine centuries. At a glance, especially from a distance, it appears that time has stood still for it. Its red sandstone walls are complete and it is still inhabited by a lord and lady, but most of it was built in the late nineteenth century and part of it has been converted into flats. The great Norman keep is virtually all that remains of the ancient castle, but even that is not the beginning of Bamburgh's history.

People sought refuge on the rock two thousand years ago and the Romans probably had a fortress and a beacon there, especially during the last days of occupation, when the coast was harried by sea raiders. In the sixth century it became the capital of King Ida the Flamebearer.

His grandson, Ethelfrith, became king of all Northumbria, and the wooden fortress became the royal capital of a kingdom which stretched from the Humber to the Forth. According to the Venerable Bede it was named Bebbanburgh in honour of Ethelfrith's wife Bebba. The Normans laid seige to it in 1095 and Matilda, Countess of Northumberland, surrendered it when William Rufus threatened to put out the eyes of her husband.

The Norman keep was built to last with walls 3.04 metres thick. It needed them, as Northumbria was a frontier zone between Scotland and England and the border was constantly disputed and fought over for centuries. When Henry V commissioned a list of fortifications in 1415, Northumberland boasted 113 pele towers and castles.

Bamburgh was the first castle in England to fall to gunfire when Edward IV turned his artillery on it during the Wars of the Roses. Artillery heralded the beginning of the end for castles as they could not hold out against it. By the end of the seventeenth century Bamburgh Castle was a virtual ruin, only the keep remained intact. During the eighteenth century it housed a girls' boarding school, which seemed an ignominious fate for a fortress site that had been a royal capital, had survived Viking and Scots invasions and had hosted King John, Henry III, Edward I and Queen Philippa. Harry Hotspur was once its Constable and Henry VI briefly made it his capital during the Wars of the Roses. It was rescued from its sad plight when the inventor and industrialist Lord Armstrong bought it in 1894.

Lord Armstrong was a remarkable man even by the standards of Victorian energy. When he bought Bamburgh he had already built Cragside, a great Victorian house also in Northumberland. It was the first house in the world to be lit by electricity that was driven by its own hydro-electricity system designed by Armstrong. At his instigation hundreds of acres of windswept moorland were transformed by planting seven million trees and shrubs on the estate. Meanwhile he had been knighted for his gun making and had made his Newcastle engineering works world famous.

The ruins of Bamburgh Castle cannot have daunted such a man at all. Indeed, the extensive restoration, building, modernization and expansion carried out on the castle was completed by 1903. Some historians dislike his renovations, believing that the Norman keep should have been left amongst the ruins. But nothing can detract from its splendour as it bestrides the rock 46 metres above the sea which washes the sands below.

Bamburgh Castle, Northumberland

'The surface of the Earth would change greatly if brick architecture were everywhere displaced by glass architecture. It would be as though the Earth clad itself in jewellery of brilliants and enamel. . . . And we should have on the earth more exquisite things than the garden of the Arabian Nights.'

PAUL SCHEERBART

Well-kept lawns and neatly trimmed hedges are commonplace in English parks and gardens, so it is not surprising to find them in the centre of the Suffolk town of Ipswich. However, although the garden shown here looks conventional, its setting is a complete surprise – witty, practical and an ingenious piece of lateral thinking. It was created for the benefit of the employees of one of the world's largest insurance brokers.

Norman Foster designed the offices of Willis, Faber, Dumas between 1970 and 1971, and created a building which constantly surprises. The low-rise structure spreads fluidly across the site like a giant amoeba, encompassing an area which used to have two streets, terraced houses, a pub and a warehouse. Its final shape and glittering black exterior have given rise to its local nickname, 'the grand piano'.

The walls are glass and the revolutionary system of glazing was researched in Belgium, Germany, France and the United States before an English company was chosen to provide the outer skin of the building. The 4,000 square metres of toughened glass is in 930 solar-tinted panes, which reflect the surrounding buildings rather like a fairground mirror, bringing jaunty life to the monochrome exterior.

The surprise on entering the building is like cracking open a black stone and finding brilliant quartz at the centre. The interior is an explosion of light and colour: open plan, bright yellow and green, and flooded with light from the glass roof which caps the restaurant on the fourth floor. A flight of glass-sided escalators cascades through the middle of the building from the roof to the ground floor. The effect is so splendidly glamorous that even the most orthodox insurance workers riding the escalator might, at any moment, break into a song and dance routine from a 1930s Hollywood musical.

But there is nothing nostalgic about the design of the building: there are roof struts of white-painted tubular steel, ceilings of polished aluminium, steel partitions in yellow, and studded green rubber flooring in the reception. Each floor radiates out from the escalators. The ground floor has a 25 metre swimming pool almost surrounded by glass, and a computerized telephone exchange; the middle two floors are open-plan office space and the top floor is a huge glass restaurant, complete with dance floor festooned with coloured lights.

Standing at the top of the escalator on the fourth floor gives a view down through the heart of the building. On the office floors there is a sea of green carpet on which desks float like bobbing boats crammed into a harbour. It appears that a lot of furniture which was not in the original design has found its way on to every floor. There is movement everywhere, people bustle continuously, but from the top floor it is a silent movie, even footsteps are deadened. The only sound, like a constant rumble of very distant thunder, comes from the escalator.

To the spectator it is rather eerie and after a while it begins to feel as if Big Brother is watching and orchestrating the workers. Before the building was designed detailed studies were made of the working needs of the 1,350 staff it had to accommodate, but even the most thoughtful designs cannot foresee every vagary of human nature. There is little privacy, and some of the staff find the building tiring to work in. In the open-plan areas people have created distinct walkways between the desks and tempers can rise if someone strays out of these into a personal work space.

Surprisingly, the garden is not used to the full. It is next to the restaurant and being overlooked by the diners seems to deter people from sitting outside, even in good weather. It seems a waste of a rather special garden, which has excellent views beyond the well-tended hedge which borders the grass.

Roof Garden, Willis, Faber, Dumas Building, Ipswich, Suffolk

'There is a rapture on the lonely shore,
There is society, where none intrudes,
By the deep sea and music in its roar:
I love not man the less, but nature more. . . .'

LORD BYRON

Suspended in an infinite sky, a pale disc of a moon holds the sea like an ethereal magnet, drawing it back to touch the sky. The world has stood still, and the haunting cries of wildfowl only accentuate the solitude. At its retreat, the moon-held sea has laid bare an acreage of ooze pocked with seawater which reflects the sky.

On England's eastern seaboard this primordial landscape is newly formed each day. The Essex coastline near the mouth of the River Blackwater is one of the loneliest and most forgotten areas of England, but once visited, it is unforgettable. South of the Blackwater Estuary the sea wall runs almost straight for miles. It keeps the sea at bay from the great sweep of flat and marshy land which was reclaimed by Dutch engineers in the seventeenth century. It is an empty landscape pierced only by remote marsh farms, cattle and the call of the curlew. On the other side of the sea wall lie great expanses of mud flats, little creeks and saltings, a haven for wildfowl.

This is a place of immense skyscapes where clouds form towering kingdoms almost as tangible as the land. The sky dominates everything and even the sea can be reduced to a silver-grey band on the horizon. Sometimes the sky is filled with storms of geese and other wildfowl who make their winter retreat here.

The Roman mercenaries, plucked from the warmth of North Africa to man the coastal fort at Bradwell, must have been discomforted at the watery emptiness of the landscape as they scanned the sea for invading Saxons. The fort was substantial but eventually abandoned and on its site rose a little Christian building of great importance.

The dauntless seventh-century missionary St Cedd landed on the Essex coast where the Blackwater empties into the North Sea. Bishop Cedd was one of four brothers, all of whom became priests. Bede records that two of them, Cedd and his brother Chad, became bishops, 'a rare thing to be met with'. Cedd was trained at that powerhouse of early English Christianity, Lindisfarne, and with characteristic vigour he built the little church of St Peter on the foundations of the wall of the Roman fort, in AD 650. The fort was a ruin but the church still stands. St Peter-on-the-Wall is a unique Saxon building, one of the oldest remaining churches in England. It stands alone, apart from a cottage, at the edge of the marshes, away from the village of Bradwell-on-Sea.

Cedd used Roman bricks from the fort to build the walls 0.6 metres thick and 7.3 metres high. The building is only 15.3 metres long and 6.7 metres wide, but this small, simple chapel has beautiful proportions and a powerful presence. It evokes the courage and single-mindedness of men like Cedd, who stormed through the Dark Ages with missionary zeal, bringing their particular light to the Saxon kingdoms. The chapel is hair-tinglingly ancient, as is the straight path to it, which follows the course of the old Roman road and has been trodden for about two thousand years. The centuries have not always been kind to St Peter-on-the-Wall. For a long time it was unrecognized and used by smugglers, and then as a barn by local farmers. Eventually its significance was realized and it was restored.

Nearby is another landmark which breaks into the vast skyline. A chunk of modern technology, Bradwell Power Station, squats beside the Blackwater. It too has a powerful and dominating presence. When it was proposed there was a chorus of disapproval, but the vast blocks can be thrilling, especially from a distance.

But the lonely saltings and mud flats sprinkled with birds are the real pull of this area. The best place to walk is on top of the sea wall, where marshes and sea stretch out on both sides and the glorious skyscapes are nearer.

LINE OF BARGES, BRADWELL-ON-SEA, ESSEX

'I remember, I remember,
The house where I was born,
The little window where the sun
Came peeping in at morn.'

THOMAS HOOD

A great lime tree straddles the skyline of a garden in Shropshire. Perched in the centre of its massive branches is England's oldest tree-house. A half-timbered cottage of dark chocolate and white, roofed with lichened tiles, it levitates among the leaves, the tranquil gaze of its ogee windows surveying farm and parkland.

This whimsical folly has been resting in its tree for at least 286 years. A map of 1714 shows it already in place, but several experts agree that it may have been there since 1692. No one knows who built it or why but it has such a quirky presence that it is easy to imagine its innovator as a woman or man of fanciful and joyous imagination.

The ancient lime tree is at least five hundred years old. It is massive and has the largest girth of any lime tree in England. After such long service it was felt that the tree deserved a rest, so it no longer bears the full weight of its delightful burden – in 1980 the tree-house was renovated and supported by steel poles. However, the lime shows little sign that it is nearing the end of its days and arboriculturalists are optimistic that it

will continue to flourish for some time.

The tree-house has enchanted many visitors. In 1832 it was visited by Victoria, the future Queen of England, when she was thirteen years old. On 27 October she wrote in her diary: 'At a little past one we walked about the grounds. I went up a staircase to a little house in a tree.'

Access to the 'little house in a tree' is still by means of a staircase. The outside of the house promises a distinctive interior and it is not a disappointment. The little white cube of a room is decorated with delicate plasterwork of fluted columns, arches, leaves and diamonds entwined with ribbons and bows. From the ceiling a goddess gazes down from a circlet of the sun's rays. It is a very special place of escape from the world. To the west, the ogee arched windows frame the surrounding countryside in a way which gives a unique sense of floating, drifting separation and peace. The view to the north is across the garden to Pitchford Hall, one of Shropshire's magnificent half-timbered houses: the protector of the tree-house.

When Victoria visited the hall in 1832

she recorded that it was '. . . a curious-looking but very comfortable house. It is striped black and white, and in the shape of a cottage.' Perhaps princesses have curious views of what constitutes a cottage as it is impossible to give Pitchford that label. It is not easily seen from the surrounding roads as it nestles beneath a bank of trees. A long drive leads to the back of the house which gives little idea of the splendour of this sixteenth-century hall, but the west-facing front is latticed with timber and pierced with many windows. The roof is gabled and topped with tall chimneys. It is impressive and welcoming at the same time.

Thomas Ottley purchased a house on the land in 1473 and his descendant built the present house, which was finished in 1549. It has never been sold. For over four hundred years it has been passed down through the family, which perhaps accounts for the richness of its interior. Lined with rich panelling, and crammed with pictures, furniture, artefacts and ghosts which have accumulated over centuries, it has the unique atmosphere of layers of history and a present-day bustling family home.

The wings of the house enfold a
beautiful garden. Emerging into it from
beneath the clock tower the eye is drawn
to the top of a steep bank, where the
tree-house perches in the ancient lime tree.
It is a symbol of escape. Others, such as
Pope and the Duchess of Suffolk, sought
their muse underground in elaborate
grottos, but at Pitchford the owner sought
inspiration and solitude in an airier clime.

Tree-house and Pitchford Hall, near Shrewsbury, Shropshire

'In the bleak, barren places fresh with unexpected graces
Leaning over rocky ledges, tenderest glances to bestow
Dauntless still in time of danger, thrilling every wayworn stranger
Scattered harebells earn a triumph never known below.'

ELAINE GOODALE

Protected from the winds which sweep across wild country, a fragile flower blooms in the lee of a massive wall. The wall was originally built to protect an empire; today it gives sanctuary to a harebell.

The vast vista of the Northumbrian moorland sustains a rich variety of plants and wildlife and it is excellent walking country. The wall climbs sinuously over the craggy edge of the Great Whin Sill, a large expanse of volcanic rock. At its highest point it reaches 375 metres above sea-level and walking along it gives spectacular views over loughs, forests and moors.

The wall was built nearly two thousand years ago. Over one million cubic yards of stone were quarried, shaped and moved into position to form a barrier to separate barbarian tribes from Roman Britain and to mark the northern limit of the Roman Empire. The decision to build the wall was made by the Emperor Hadrian when he visited this desolate corner of his empire in AD 122. It took about eight years to build and when it was finished it stretched from sea to sea across the narrowest part of England, 80 Roman miles (over 117 kilometres) from Wallsend in the east to Bowness-on-Solway in the west.

Hadrian's Wall served as an enduring boundary for a mighty empire for 260 years and remains a monument to the skill of its engineers and builders. Much of it still stands and in places it is almost its original height of 4.6 metres. To the east the wall was built of stone, but to the west it was of turf construction. There were stone mile castles every Roman mile and signalling turrets in between. It was rebuilt in AD 200 and is thought to have been limewashed. To the northern tribes it must have been an awe-inspiring reminder of the might of Rome. It was finally abandoned when Rome was threatened by Goths, Vandals and Huns, and Roman troops were recalled to protect the hub of the empire.

Roman auxiliaries named the desolate country north of Hadrian's Wall *Ad Fines* – The End of the World. To be posted there was regarded as a penance by many of the soldiers who manned it. Facing a Northumbrian winter and the marauding bands of barbarians who launched attacks on the wall from the north must have been grim for even the most hardened old campaigners.

There were some consolations: efforts were made to bring some of the comforts of Roman life to this bleak outpost. Although the countryside around is desolate, at the time of the occupation the forts on the wall must have thronged with life. There were 13,000 infantry and 5,500 cavalry deployed along the length of the wall. The fort at Housesteads, one of the wall's seventeen large forts, contained 1,000 infantry. Here there were soldiers' bath houses with steam rooms and baths. There were also granaries, latrines, stables, a headquarters, and barrack blocks with cooking facilities. Officers had separate quarters. The Romans brought their gods with them: excavations along the wall have revealed temples to Mithras and Jupiter, while German auxiliaries were allowed to practice their own form of worship. It seems that local deities were worshipped too.

Such bustle attracted local entrepreneurs. South of the major forts settlements of huts sprang up where traders, tavern keepers and camp-followers plied their trade. All life was there: an unscrupulous gambler's loaded dice, a forger's mould, and murder victims have been found. An invitation to the birthday party of the commanding officer's wife was discovered in one of the earliest forts.

Trade flowed from overseas – the wine for birthday parties, along with glass, pottery, corn and cloth must have arrived at the mouth of the Tyne. But perhaps the most exotic and extraordinary import was brought by a merchant of the caravan city of Palmyra in Syria, who travelled to the edge of the Roman Empire to sell silk for the banners of the cavalry units based on Hadrian's Wall. The silk had travelled even further, as China was the only source of this fabric, a fragile emblem of the protectors of Hadrian's mighty wall.

HADRIAN'S WALL LOOKING EAST TOWARDS MILE CASTLE 37

LOCATIONS

1   MONTACUTE HOUSE, SOMERSET

2   THE COWS, MILTON KEYNES, BUCKINGHAMSHIRE

3   THE GROTTO AND MARSDEN ROCK, TYNE AND WEAR

4   ROCHE ROCK, ROCHE, CORNWALL

5   WINCHESTER CATHEDRAL, HAMPSHIRE

6   THE OLD WELLINGTON INN, MANCHESTER

7   COMPOSITE SIGNALS ORGANIZATION STATION, MORWENSTOW, CORNWALL

8   PUBLIC TELEPHONE, GUITING POWER, GLOUCESTERSHIRE

9   HOOVER FACTORY, PERIVALE, MIDDLESEX

10 LAVENDER FARM, HEACHAM, NORFOLK

11 TRIPLE BRIDGE, CROWLAND, LINCOLNSHIRE

12 STONE CIRCLE, AVEBURY, WILTSHIRE

13 THE LIGHTHOUSE, SOUTHWOLD, SUFFOLK

14 THE THAMES, TWICKENHAM, MIDDLESEX

15 SEVEN ROCK POINT, NEAR LYME REGIS, DORSET

16 HANAFIA MOSQUE, MANNINGHAM, BRADFORD, YORKSHIRE

17 THE MAZE, GLENDURGAN GARDENS, CORNWALL

18 HARDWICK HALL, DERBYSHIRE

19 LINDISFARNE CASTLE, HOLY ISLAND, NORTHUMBERLAND

20 THE ROYAL LIVER BUILDING, LIVERPOOL

21 MALHAM COVE, YORKSHIRE

22 TOWER MILL, POLEGATE, SUSSEX

23 BARTON AQUEDUCT AND MANCHESTER SHIP CANAL

24 THE TEN COMMANDMENTS STONE, DARTMOOR, DEVON

25 SAMUEL GAWITH'S SNUFF MILL, KENDAL, CUMBRIA

26 BAMBURGH CASTLE, NORTHUMBERLAND

27 ROOF GARDEN, WILLIS, FABER, DUMAS BUILDING, IPSWICH, SUFFOLK

28 BRADWELL-ON-SEA, ESSEX

29 TREE-HOUSE AND PITCHFORD HALL, NEAR SHREWSBURY, SHROPSHIRE

30 HADRIAN'S WALL, NORTHUMBERLAND

NEWCASTLE-
UPON-TYNE

LEEDS

NORWICH

BIRMINGHAM

LONDON

BRISTOL

EXETER

FATHER TIME, THE SOUTHGATE CLOCK, GLOUCESTER

ACKNOWLEDGEMENTS

Many thanks to the following people who helped us so generously with their knowledge and time:

Diana Pierce of Polegate Windmill; Henry Head of Norfolk Lavender; Miss Silberberg of Gunnersbury Museum; Les Collins of Hoover Trading Co.; Tony Eggs of Tesco; Yvonne Sylvester; the boys and girls of Guiting Power who helped with the cat; Jim Crow, Norma Skeels and Angela Hall with the Landrover at Hadrian's Wall; Graham Forest, Mr Harris and everyone at Samuel Gawith; Mrs Brogden of The Old Wellington; the crew at Barton Aqueduct; Mr Nishter of the Hanafia Mosque; Tim Smith of Bradford Industrial Museum; Diana Lanham and everyone who helped us at The National Trust; David Price and the children of Ewelme School; Stanley Hale; Ann Walton of the Liverpool Tourist Office; Paul McKay of the Royal Liver Friendly Society; Gordon Read of Liverpool Museum; Carol Folley of St Austell; The Revd N.H. Toogood, Rector of Roche; Mrs Bawden of the Philpot Museum, Lyme Regis; Mr and Mrs Barry Rose of Stowe Barton Farm; Mr and Mrs Oliver Colthurst of Pitchford Hall; David Mounce and Mr and Mrs Mike Lawson of Montacute House; J.C.H. Phelips Esq.; John Hardacre, Curator of Winchester Cathedral; Ted Enever of Milton Keynes Development Corporation; George Hague of Hardwick Hall; Mr Stephens, Public Relations, Willis, Faber, Dumas; Karen Plumstead of British Telecom; Tony Fisher of the Sole Bay Inn; and everyone who sheltered us from the rain and gave us cups of tea.

Our thanks also to the many friends who patiently listened to our ramblings and encouraged and supported us throughout the project, especially: Ari Ashley; Andrew Bicknell; Martin Dohrn; everyone at Embankment Studios; Celia Forestal; Barbara Gilgallon; Ginny Grub; Suzanne Haines; Andrea Nixon; George Seddon; Janet Slingsby; Maureen Walker; and our Thermos; the tripod; the Fuji panoramic camera; the word processor, the mighty Citroën diesel engine; and Mackie.

Finally our thanks to Peter Clifford and his team at Alan Sutton whose enthusiasm and encouragement made it all possible.